ELEMENTARY ALGEBRA

Grades 3 - 4

D1609305

by Marcia Dana

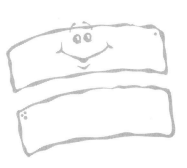

Carson-Dellosa Publishing Company, Inc.
Greensboro, North Carolina

Credits

Editor: Amy Gamble

Layout Design: Tia

Inside Illustrations:

Cover Design: Anne

Cover Illustrations:

Prufrock Press 1 hr. mysteries

Dr. Funster's Creative Thinky Putterzes .

ISBN 1-59441-193-X

Table of Contents

Introduction 4

Understanding Patterns
Extending Patterns...5
Describing Patterns 10
Transforming Patterns 12
Skip Counting 13
Addition Patterns 22
Subtraction Patterns 27
Mixed Patterns 30
Multiples and Factors 33
Functions 38

Representing Mathematical Situations
Equality and Inequality 48
Equality..51
Differences 55
Translating Word Problems 59
Solving Word Problems..62
Writing Word Problems 64

Using Mathematical Models
Writing Number Sentences 65
Mathematical Relationships 82
Solving Number Sentences 98
Equality..103

Investigating Change... 108

Using Variables.. 114

Answer Key 120

Introduction

This book focuses on many of the early algebra concepts described in the NCTM Algebra strand. The activities in this book are designed to expand students' mathematical understanding, particularly in the area of algebra. A variety of developmentally appropriate activities will help students become familiar with the following elementary algebra skills:

- number and shape patterns
- skip counting
- functions
- equality and inequality
- comparing sets
- writing number sentences
- solving number sentences
- properties of numbers
- mathematical situations
- investigating change using graphs and tables
- variables

Each concept is presented in an easy-to-understand way that is intended to be both interesting and fun for students. This book can be a valuable tool in helping students achieve growth in their mathematical development.

Name _____   Date _____

Dinosaur Teeth Patterns

Directions:

Shade the "teeth" to continue each pattern.

1.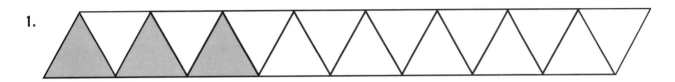

2.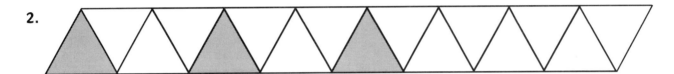

3.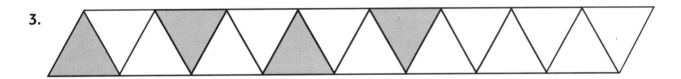

4.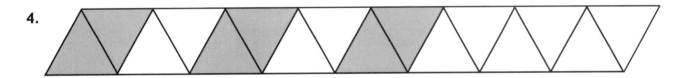

5.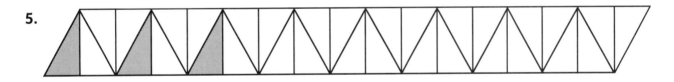

6.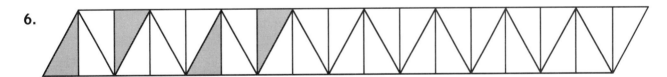

7.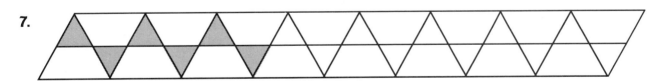

8.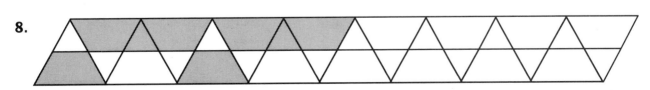

Alphabet Squares

Extending Patterns

Directions:

Fill all of the squares to continue each pattern.

1. | S | T | T | S | T | T | S | T | T | | | | | | |

2. | C | D | D | D | C | D | D | D | | | | | | | |

3. | X | X | Y | Y | X | X | Y | Y | | | | | | | |

4. | J | J | J | K | K | J | J | J | K | K | | | | | |

5. | O | P | P | P | P | P | O | P | P | P | P | P | | | |

6. | G | G | G | H | G | G | G | H | | | | | | | |

7. | M | N | N | O | O | O | M | N | N | O | O | O | | | |

8. | U | U | V | W | W | U | U | V | W | W | | | | | |

9. | A | B | B | B | B | C | A | B | B | B | B | C | | | |

10. | P | P | P | P | Q | R | P | P | P | P | Q | R | | | |

Growing Patterns

Directions:
Fill in the blanks to continue each pattern.

1. 1 1 2 2 3 3 4 4 5 5 ___ ___ ___ ___ ___ ___ ___ ___ ___ ___

2. 1 1 2 3 3 4 5 5 6 ___ ___ ___ ___ ___ ___ ___ ___ ___

3. 1 2 2 2 3 4 4 4 5 6 6 6 ___ ___ ___ ___ ___ ___ ___ ___ ___

4. 1 1 1 2 3 3 3 4 5 5 5 6 ___ ___ ___ ___ ___ ___ ___ ___

5. 1 1 1 2 2 3 3 3 4 4 ___ ___ ___ ___ ___ ___ ___ ___ ___

6. 1 1 2 2 2 2 3 3 4 4 4 ___ ___ ___ ___ ___ ___ ___ ___ ___

7. 1 2 2 3 3 4 5 5 6 6 7 8 8 9 9 ___ ___ ___ ___ ___ ___ ___ ___

8. 1 1 1 2 2 3 4 4 4 5 5 6 ___ ___ ___ ___ ___ ___ ___ ___

9. 1 2 2 3 4 5 5 6 7 8 8 9 ___ ___ ___ ___ ___ ___ ___

10. 1 2 2 3 3 3 4 5 5 6 6 6 ___ ___ ___ ___ ___ ___ ___ ___

Name _____   Date _____

Directions:
Each of these triangle patterns involves some movement. Figure out what is moving and how to show the next part of the pattern.

Draw the next triangle.

1.

2.

3.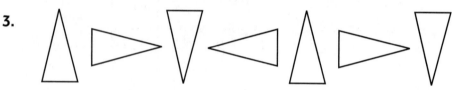

4.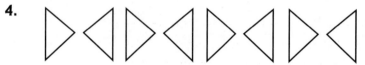

Mark or shade the next triangle.

5.

6.

7.

8.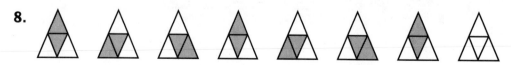

Name _____   Date _____

Hidden Patterns

Directions:
The patterns below are hidden in the hundred chart. Find them and continue each pattern.

1	2	3	4	5	6	7	8	9	10
11	12	13	14	15	16	17	18	19	20
21	22	23	24	25	26	27	28	29	30
31	32	33	34	35	36	37	38	39	40
41	42	43	44	45	46	47	48	49	50
51	52	53	54	55	56	57	58	59	60
61	62	63	64	65	66	67	68	69	70
71	72	73	74	75	76	77	78	79	80
81	82	83	84	85	86	87	88	89	90
91	92	93	94	95	96	97	98	99	100

1. 1, 3, 5, 7, 9, 11, _____, _____, _____, _____, _____, _____

2. 2, 4, 6, 8, 10, 12, _____, _____, _____, _____, _____, _____

3. 5, 10, 15, 20, 25, _____, _____, _____, _____, _____, _____

4. 10, 20, 30, 40, _____, _____, _____, _____, _____, _____

5. 1, 11, 21, 31, 41, _____, _____, _____, _____, _____

6. 1, 12, 23, 34, 45, _____, _____, _____, _____, _____

7. 7, 17, 27, 37, 47, _____, _____, _____, _____, _____

8. 10, 19, 28, 37, 46, _____, _____, _____, _____, _____

Name _____   Date _____

How Do They Work?

Directions:
Draw or write the next part of each pattern. Then, describe how it works.

1.   _____

   Describe this pattern. _____

   _____

2. G H H I I I J K K L L L ___ ___ ___ ___ ___ ___ ___

   Describe this pattern. _____

   _____

3. △ △ ▽ ▽ △ △ ▽ ▽ ___ ___ ___ ___

   Describe this pattern. _____

   _____

4. 9, 18, 27, 36, 45, 54, 63, 72, 81, 90, _____, _____

   Describe this pattern. _____

   _____

5. 2, 3, 5, 6, 8, 9, 11, 12, 14, 15, _____, _____

   Describe this pattern. _____

   _____

Kinds of Patterns

Directions:
Continue the pattern. Then, answer the questions about the pattern.

○ ○ □ ○ ○ □ ○ ○ □ ___ ___ ___

1. How does this pattern work? _____

_____

2. Which of these patterns is the same kind? Circle it.

ABCABCABC

AABAABAAB

AABBAABBAABB

3. How is this pattern the same kind? _____

_____

● ●

○ △ □ ○ △ □ ○ △ □ ___ ___ ___

4. How does this pattern work? _____

_____

5. Which of these patterns is the same kind? Circle it.

ABBABBABB

ABCCABCCABCC

ABCABCABC

6. How is this pattern the same kind? _____

_____

Make Your Own Patterns

Transforming Patterns

Directions:

Make five letter patterns. Make each one different. Then, make five number patterns using the same patterns as the letter patterns.

Letter Patterns

1. ____ ____ ____ ____ ____ ____ ____ ____ ____ ____

2. ____ ____ ____ ____ ____ ____ ____ ____ ____ ____

3. ____ ____ ____ ____ ____ ____ ____ ____ ____ ____

4. ____ ____ ____ ____ ____ ____ ____ ____ ____ ____

5. ____ ____ ____ ____ ____ ____ ____ ____ ____ ____

Number Patterns

1. ____ ____ ____ ____ ____ ____ ____ ____ ____ ____

2. ____ ____ ____ ____ ____ ____ ____ ____ ____ ____

3. ____ ____ ____ ____ ____ ____ ____ ____ ____ ____

4. ____ ____ ____ ____ ____ ____ ____ ____ ____ ____

5. ____ ____ ____ ____ ____ ____ ____ ____ ____ ____

Name _____   Date _____

Counting Dots

Directions:
Count by 2s and 3s. Draw the dots in the boxes. Write the total numbers underneath.

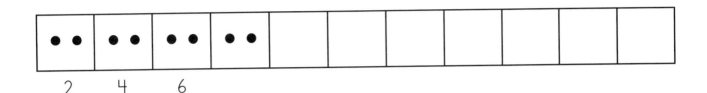

2   4   6

1. How much is 2 boxes of 2s? _____

2. How much is 7 boxes of 2s? _____

3. How much would 12 boxes of 2s make? _____

4. How many boxes of 2s make 16? _____

5. How many boxes of 2s make 22? _____

6. How many boxes of 2s would make 30? _____

. . . .

3   6   9

7. How much is 4 boxes of 3s? _____

8. How much is 9 boxes of 3s? _____

9. How much would 12 boxes of 3s make? _____

10. How many boxes of 3s make 24? _____

11. How many boxes of 3s make 33? _____

12. How many boxes of 3s would make 39? _____

Name _____   Date _____

Counting Freckles

Directions:

Count by 4s and 5s. Draw the freckles in the boxes. Write the total numbers underneath.

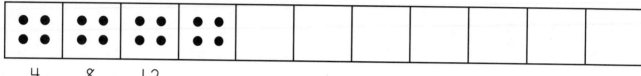

4   8   12

1. How much is 4 boxes of 4s? _____

2. How much is 8 boxes of 4s? _____

3. How much would 13 boxes of 4s make? _____

4. How many boxes of 4s make 20? _____

5. How many boxes of 4s make 36? _____

6. How many boxes of 4s would make 48? _____

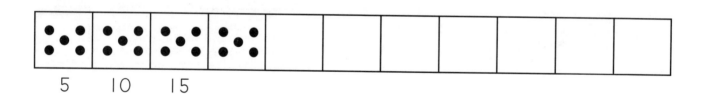

5   10   15

7. How much is 6 boxes of 5s? _____

8. How much is 10 boxes of 5s? _____

9. How much would 12 boxes of 5s make? _____

10. How many boxes of 5s make 45? _____

11. How many boxes of 5s make 55? _____

12. How many boxes of 5s would make 70? _____

Name _____   Date _____

Counting Specks

Directions:
Count by 6s and 7s. Draw the specks in the boxes. Write the total numbers underneath.

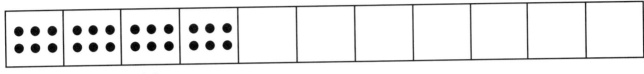

6   12   18

1. How much is 5 boxes of 6s? _____

2. How much is 11 boxes of 6s? _____

3. How much would 12 boxes of 6s make? _____

4. How many boxes of 6s make 42? _____

5. How many boxes of 6s make 54? _____

6. How many boxes of 6s would make 78? _____

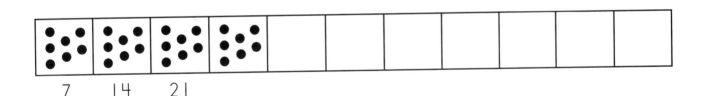

7   14   21

7. How much is 5 boxes of 7s? _____

8. How much is 8 boxes of 7s? _____

9. How much would 12 boxes of 7s make? _____

10. How many boxes of 7s make 49? _____

11. How many boxes of 7s make 63? _____

12. How many boxes of 7s would make 98? _____

Name _____ Date _____

Counting Crumbs

Directions:
Count by 8s and 9s. Draw the crumbs in the boxes. Write the total numbers underneath.

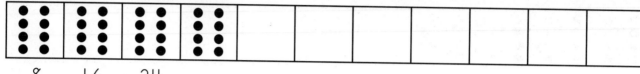

8   16   24

1. How much is 6 boxes of 8s? _____

2. How much is 10 boxes of 8s? _____

3. How much would 12 boxes of 8s make? _____

4. How many boxes of 8s make 40? _____

5. How many boxes of 8s make 88? _____

6. How many boxes of 8s would make 104? _____

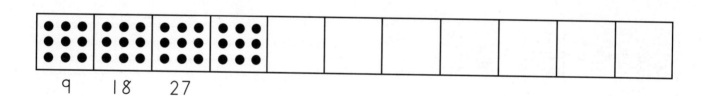

9   18   27

7. How much is 5 boxes of 9s? _____

8. How much is 7 boxes of 9s? _____

9. How much would 12 boxes of 9s make? _____

10. How many boxes of 9s make 72? _____

11. How many boxes of 9s make 81? _____

12. How many boxes of 9s would make 117? _____

Name _____   Date _____

Counting Periods

Directions:
Count by 10s and 11s. Draw the periods in the boxes. Write the total numbers underneath.

10   20   30

1. How much is 8 boxes of 10s? _____

2. How much is 11 boxes of 10s? _____

3. How much would 13 boxes of 10s make? _____

4. How many boxes of 10s make 90? _____

5. How many boxes of 10s make 100? _____

6. How many boxes of 10s would make 120? _____

• •

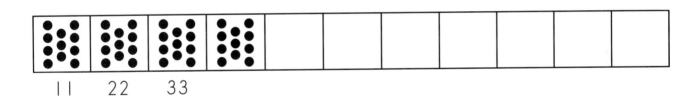

11   22   33

7. How much is 7 boxes of 11s? _____

8. How much is 10 boxes of 11s? _____

9. How much would 12 boxes of 11s make? _____

10. How many boxes of 11s make 99? _____

11. How many boxes of 11s make 121? _____

12. How many boxes of 11s would make 143? _____

Make Your Own Times Table

Skip Counting

Directions:

Fill in the answers on the times table below. Then, circle "odd," "even," or "both" to describe the patterns in the table.

x	1	2	3	4	5	6	7	8	9	10
1										
2										
3										
4										
5										
6										
7										
8										
9										
10										

1. Count by ones.   odd   even   both

2. Count by twos.   odd   even   both

3. Count by threes.   odd   even   both

4. Count by fours.   odd   even   both

5. Count by fives.   odd   even   both

6. Count by sixes.   odd   even   both

7. Count by sevens.   odd   even   both

8. Count by eights.   odd   even   both

9. Count by nines.   odd   even   both

10. Count by tens.   odd   even   both

Name _____   Date _____

Lulu Makes Change

Directions:
Lulu works at her mother's store. She made some charts to help her make change. Fill in the charts.
Then, answer the questions below.

Dimes to Nickels

Dimes	1	2	3	4	5	6	7	8	9	10
Nickels	2									

Quarters to Nickels

Quarters	1	2	3	4	5	6	7	8	9	10
Nickels	5									

Dollars to Quarters

Dollars	1	2	3	4	5	6	7	8	9	10
Quarters	4									

Dollars to Dimes

Dollars	1	2	3	4	5	6	7	8	9	10
Dimes	10									

Dollars to Nickels

Dollars	1	2	3	4	5	6	7	8	9	10
Nickels	20									

1. How many nickels are 8 dimes worth? _____

2. How many nickels are 6 quarters worth? _____

3. How many quarters are 4 dollars worth? _____

4. How many dimes are 7 dollars worth? _____

5. How many nickels are 5 dollars worth? _____

Name _____   Date _____

Money Families

Directions:

Tell how much money each person has.

The Nickel Family

1. Nick has 8 nickels. _____ ¢ or $_____

2. Norm has 12 nickels. _____ ¢ or $_____

3. Nichole has 20 nickels. _____ ¢ or $_____

4. Ned has 30 nickels. _____ ¢ or $_____

5. Nancy has 100 nickels. _____ ¢ or $_____

The Dime Family

6. Dina has 6 dimes. _____ ¢ or $_____

7. Dennis has 10 dimes. _____ ¢ or $_____

8. Desmond has 15 dimes. _____ ¢ or $_____

9. Delia has 20 dimes. _____ ¢ or $_____

10. Daria has 100 dimes. _____ ¢ or $_____

The Quarter Family

11. Quentin has 3 quarters. _____ ¢ or $_____

12. Quisha has 6 quarters. _____ ¢ or $_____

13. Quincy has 8 quarters. _____ ¢ or $_____

14. Quayle has 20 quarters. _____ ¢ or $_____

15. Quinna has 100 quarters. _____ ¢ or $_____

Name _____   Date _____

Directions:
The crazy clown cousins want to figure out how much money they each have. Write the amounts for each type of coin and add to find the total. Then, answer the questions below.

Example:

Egbert has 3 nickels   _15_ ¢

and 2 dimes.   _20_ ¢

How much in all?   _35_ ¢

1. Doofus has 6 nickels   _____ ¢

    and 5 dimes.   _____ ¢

    How much in all?   _____ ¢

2. Ninny has 10 nickels   _____ ¢

    and 4 dimes.   _____ ¢

    How much in all?   _____ ¢

3. Twerpy has 4 nickels   _____ ¢

    and 2 quarters.   _____ ¢

    How much in all?   _____ ¢

4. Goofus has 2 nickels   _____ ¢

    and 2 dimes   _____ ¢

    and 2 quarters.   _____ ¢

    How much in all?   _____ ¢

5. Bozo has 3 nickels   _____ ¢

    and 3 dimes   _____ ¢

    and 2 quarters.   _____ ¢

    How much in all?   _____ ¢

6. Who has the largest amount of money? _____

7. Which 2 cousins have the same amount of money?

    _____

8. How much more does Bozo have than Egbert? _____

9. How much less does Goofus have than Ninny? _____

10. Who has twice as much money as Egbert? _____

Name _____ Date _____

Plenty of Plus Patterns

Directions:
Many patterns can be made by adding the same number over and over. Look at the example, then complete the patterns below.

Example: **+2 Pattern**

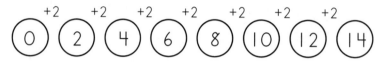

1.   **+1 Pattern**

2.   **+2 Pattern**

3.   **+3 Pattern**

4.   **+3 Pattern**

5.   **+3 Pattern**

6.   **+4 Pattern**

Name _____   Date _____

Plenty More Plus Patterns

Directions:
Complete these patterns.

1. **+4 Pattern**

2. **+4 Pattern**

3. **+4 Pattern**

4. **+5 Pattern**

5. **+6 Pattern**

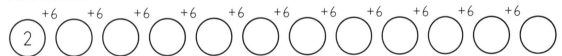

6. **+7 Pattern**

7. **+8 Pattern**

8. **+9 Pattern**

Name _____   Date _____

Whoppers!

Directions:
Figure out what each plus pattern is and continue it.

1.   +_____ **Pattern**

2.   +_____ **Pattern**

3.   +_____ **Pattern**

4.   +_____ **Pattern**

5.   +_____ **Pattern**

6.   +_____ **Pattern**

7.   +_____ **Pattern**

8.   +_____ **Pattern**

Name _____ Date _____

Directions:
Sometimes two plus patterns get together and make a new pattern. Look at the example, then complete the patterns below.

Example: **+1, +3 Pattern**

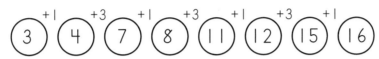

1.   **+1, +4 Pattern**

2.   **+2, +3 Pattern**

3.   **+2, +5 Pattern**

4.   **+1, +10 Pattern**

+1 +10 +1 +10 +1 +10 +1 +10 +1 +10 +1
(1)(2)(12)(13)( )( )( )( )( )( )( )( )

5.   **+3, +6 Pattern**

+3 +6 +3 +6 +3 +6 +3 +6 +3 +6 +3
(1)(4)(10)(13)( )( )( )( )( )( )( )( )

6.   **+5, +10 Pattern**

+5 +10 +5 +10 +5 +10 +5 +10 +5 +10 +5
(5)(10)(20)(25)( )( )( )( )( )( )( )( )

Name ______________________________ Date ______________

Name That Pattern

Addition Patterns

Directions:
Tell what plus pattern or plus pattern pal is used in each pattern below.

1.	+_____	3	8	13	18	23	28	33	38
2.	+_____	7	9	11	13	15	17	19	21
3.	+_____	10	13	16	19	22	25	28	31
4.	+_____	34	44	54	64	74	84	94	104
5.	+_____	2	10	18	26	34	42	50	58
6.	+_____, +_____	1	4	6	9	11	14	16	19
7.	+_____, +_____	0	1	6	7	12	13	18	19
8.	+_____, +_____	3	7	9	13	15	19	21	25
9.	+_____, +_____	5	15	17	27	29	39	41	51
10.	+_____, +_____	0	5	25	30	50	55	75	80

Name _____ Date _____

Many Minus Patterns

Directions:
Many patterns can be made by subtracting the same number over and over. Look at the example, then complete the patterns below.

Example: -2 Pattern

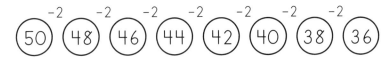

1. **-1 Pattern**

2. **-2 Pattern**

3. **-3 Pattern**

4. **-4 Pattern**

5. **-5 Pattern**

6. **-6 Pattern**

Name That Pattern Again

Subtraction Patterns

Directions:

Figure out what each minus pattern is and continue it.

1.   -_____ **Pattern**

2.   -_____ **Pattern**

3.   -_____ **Pattern**

4.   -_____ **Pattern**

5.   -_____ **Pattern**

6.   -_____ **Pattern**

7.   -_____ **Pattern**

8.   -_____ **Pattern**

Elementary Algebra • CD-104105

Name _____   Date _____

Minus Pattern Pals

Subtraction Patterns

Directions:

Sometimes two minus patterns get together and make a new pattern. Look at the example, then complete the patterns below.

Example: − 1, − 2 Pattern

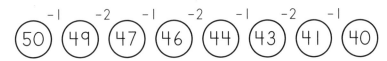

1. **− 2, − 3 Pattern**

2. **− 1, − 5 Pattern**

3. **− 4, − 3 Pattern**

4. **− 5, − 10 Pattern**

5. **− 2, − 4 Pattern**

6. **− 10, − 20 Pattern**

Name _____   Date _____

Directions:

Sometimes a plus pattern and a minus pattern get together and make a new pattern. Look at the example, then complete the patterns below.

Example: +2, - 1 Pattern

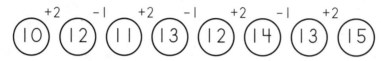

1.   **+3, - 1 Pattern**

2.   **+5, -2 Pattern**

3.   **- 1, +4 Pattern**

4.   **-2, + 10 Pattern**

5.   **-3, +6 Pattern**

6.   **+5, - 10 Pattern**

Name _____   Date _____

Secret Pattern Pals

Directions:

Tell what pattern pals are used in each pattern below. Be sure to tell which are plus and which are minus.

1. _____, _____   ⃝20 ⃝22 ⃝19 ⃝21 ⃝18 ⃝20 ⃝17 ⃝19

2. _____, _____   ⃝50 ⃝51 ⃝46 ⃝47 ⃝42 ⃝43 ⃝38 ⃝39

3. _____, _____   ⃝5 ⃝8 ⃝7 ⃝10 ⃝9 ⃝12 ⃝11 ⃝14

4. _____, _____   ⃝2 ⃝6 ⃝4 ⃝8 ⃝6 ⃝10 ⃝8 ⃝12

5. _____, _____   ⃝6 ⃝5 ⃝10 ⃝9 ⃝14 ⃝13 ⃝18 ⃝17

6. _____, _____   ⃝8 ⃝6 ⃝9 ⃝7 ⃝10 ⃝8 ⃝11 ⃝9

7. _____, _____   ⃝30 ⃝25 ⃝27 ⃝22 ⃝24 ⃝19 ⃝21 ⃝16

8. _____, _____   ⃝80 ⃝70 ⃝72 ⃝62 ⃝64 ⃝54 ⃝56 ⃝46

9. _____, _____   ⃝25 ⃝21 ⃝30 ⃝26 ⃝35 ⃝31 ⃝40 ⃝36

10. _____, _____   ⃝3 ⃝10 ⃝8 ⃝15 ⃝13 ⃝20 ⃝18 ⃝25

Make Your Own Pattern Pals

Directions:

Choose your own pattern pals and make patterns. Remember to name your patterns.

1. _____ , _____ ◯ ◯ ◯ ◯ ◯ ◯ ◯ ◯

2. _____ , _____ ◯ ◯ ◯ ◯ ◯ ◯ ◯ ◯

3. _____ , _____ ◯ ◯ ◯ ◯ ◯ ◯ ◯ ◯

4. _____ , _____ ◯ ◯ ◯ ◯ ◯ ◯ ◯ ◯

5. _____ , _____ ◯ ◯ ◯ ◯ ◯ ◯ ◯ ◯

6. _____ , _____ ◯ ◯ ◯ ◯ ◯ ◯ ◯ ◯

7. _____ , _____ ◯ ◯ ◯ ◯ ◯ ◯ ◯ ◯

8. _____ , _____ ◯ ◯ ◯ ◯ ◯ ◯ ◯ ◯

9. _____ , _____ ◯ ◯ ◯ ◯ ◯ ◯ ◯ ◯

10. _____ , _____ ◯ ◯ ◯ ◯ ◯ ◯ ◯ ◯

All About 8

Multiples and Factors

Directions:

Circle the blocks to make groups. Note which groups come out even.

1. Group by ones.   ☐ ☐ ☐ ☐ ☐ ☐ ☐ ☐   Does it come out even?
_____

2. Group by twos.   ☐ ☐ ☐ ☐ ☐ ☐ ☐ ☐   Does it come out even?
_____

3. Group by threes.   ☐ ☐ ☐ ☐ ☐ ☐ ☐ ☐   Does it come out even?
_____

4. Group by fours.   ☐ ☐ ☐ ☐ ☐ ☐ ☐ ☐   Does it come out even?
_____

5. Group by fives.   ☐ ☐ ☐ ☐ ☐ ☐ ☐ ☐   Does it come out even?
_____

6. Group by sixes.   ☐ ☐ ☐ ☐ ☐ ☐ ☐ ☐   Does it come out even?
_____

7. Group by sevens.   ☐ ☐ ☐ ☐ ☐ ☐ ☐ ☐   Does it come out even?
_____

8. Group by eights.   ☐ ☐ ☐ ☐ ☐ ☐ ☐ ☐   Does it come out even?
_____

9. Which numbers can you group 8 by and come out even?

_____, _____, _____, and _____

These numbers are called **factors** of 8;

8 is called a **multiple** of these numbers.

So, 8 is a **multiple** of 1, 2, 4, and 8.

And, 1, 2, 4, and 8 are **factors** of 8.

All About 12

Directions:
Circle the Xs to make groups. Note which groups come out even.

1. Group by ones. X X X X X X X X X X X X Does it come out even? _____	**2.** Group by twos. X X X X X X X X X X X X Does it come out even? _____
3. Group by threes. X X X X X X X X X X X X Does it come out even? _____	**4.** Group by fours. X X X X X X X X X X X X Does it come out even? _____
5. Group by fives. X X X X X X X X X X X X Does it come out even? _____	**6.** Group by sixes. X X X X X X X X X X X X Does it come out even? _____
7. Group by sevens. X X X X X X X X X X X X Does it come out even? _____	**8.** Group by eights. X X X X X X X X X X X X Does it come out even? _____
9. Group by nines. X X X X X X X X X X X X Does it come out even? _____	**10.** Group by tens. X X X X X X X X X X X X Does it come out even? _____
11.. Group by elevens. X X X X X X X X X X X X Does it come out even? _____	**12.** Group by twelves. X X X X X X X X X X X X Does it come out even? _____

13. Which numbers can you group 12 by and come out even?

_____, _____, _____, _____, _____, and _____ are **factors** of 12.

14. Write multiplication sentences about the factors of 12.

_____ x _____ = 12   _____ x _____ = 12   _____ x _____ = 12

_____ x _____ = 12   _____ x _____ = 12   _____ x _____ = 12

15. 12 is a **multiple** of _____, _____, _____, _____, _____, and _____.

Factors

Multiples and Factors

Directions:
Use the multiplication table to help answer the questions below.

x	1	2	3	4	5	6	7	8	9	10
1	1	2	3	4	5	6	7	8	9	10
2	2	4	6	8	10	12	14	16	18	20
3	3	6	9	12	15	18	21	24	27	30
4	4	8	12	16	20	24	28	32	36	40
5	5	10	15	20	25	30	35	40	45	50
6	6	12	18	24	30	36	42	48	54	60
7	7	14	21	28	35	42	49	56	63	70
8	8	16	24	32	40	48	56	64	72	80
9	9	18	27	36	45	54	63	72	81	90
10	10	20	30	40	50	60	70	80	90	100

1. Is 6 a factor of 30? _____   Is 6 a factor of 49? _____

2. Is 3 a factor of 16? _____   Is 3 a factor of 21? _____

3. Is 4 a factor of 32? _____   Is 4 a factor of 40? _____

4. Is 5 a factor of 15? _____   Is 5 a factor of 42? _____

5. Is 8 a factor of 63? _____   Is 8 a factor of 40? _____

6. Is 9 a factor of 45? _____   Is 9 a factor of 49? _____

7. Name 4 factors of 18. _____ _____ _____ _____

8. Name 4 factors of 24. _____ _____ _____ _____

Name _____   Date _____

Multiples

Directions:

Use the multiplication table to help answer the questions below.

x	1	2	3	4	5	6	7	8	9	10
1	1	2	3	4	5	6	7	8	9	10
2	2	4	6	8	10	12	14	16	18	20
3	3	6	9	12	15	18	21	24	27	30
4	4	8	12	16	20	24	28	32	36	40
5	5	10	15	20	25	30	35	40	45	50
6	6	12	18	24	30	36	42	48	54	60
7	7	14	21	28	35	42	49	56	63	70
8	8	16	24	32	40	48	56	64	72	80
9	9	18	27	36	45	54	63	72	81	90
10	10	20	30	40	50	60	70	80	90	100

1. Is 35 a multiple of 7? _____   Is 35 a multiple of 9? _____

2. Is 27 a multiple of 3? _____   Is 27 a multiple of 5? _____

3. Is 28 a multiple of 7? _____   Is 28 a multiple of 4? _____

4. Is 56 a multiple of 9? _____   Is 56 a multiple of 7? _____

5. Is 42 a multiple of 6? _____   Is 42 a multiple of 8? _____

6. Is 24 a multiple of 6? _____   Is 24 a multiple of 8? _____

7. Name 6 multiples of 5. _____ _____ _____ _____ _____ _____

8. Name 6 multiples of 9. _____ _____ _____ _____ _____ _____

Multiple Riddles

Multiples and Factors

Directions:
Fill in the multiplication table. Then, use the table to help answer the riddles below.

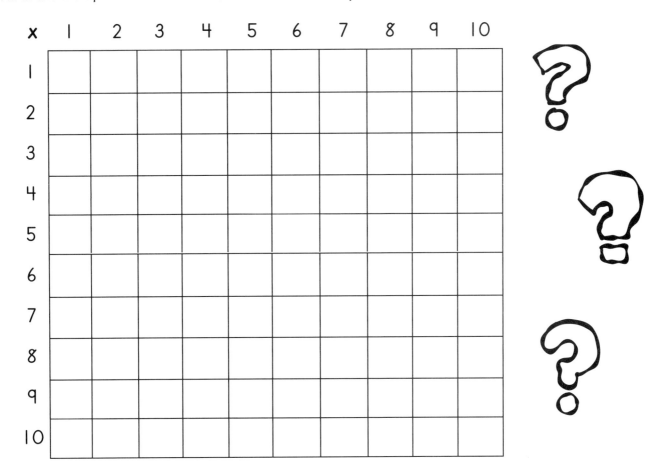

1. I am a multiple of 5. I am even.
   I am greater than 15. I am less than 30.

   Who am I? _____

2. I am a multiple of 3. I am odd.
   I am less than 20. I am greater than 10.

   Who am I? _____

3. I am a multiple of 7. I am odd.
   I am greater than 30. I am less than 45.

   Who am I? _____

4. I am a multiple of 4. I am even.
   I am greater than 30. I am less than 36.

   Who am I? _____

5. I am a multiple of 9. I am even.
   I am greater than 50. I am less than 70.

   Who am I? _____

6. I am a multiple of 8. I am even.
   I am less than 80. I am greater than 65.

   Who am I? _____

Name _____   Date _____

A Lot of Legs

Directions:
Complete each chart about animal legs. Then, use the charts to answer the questions below.

Birds

number of birds	number of legs
1	2
2	
3	
4	
5	
6	

Cats

number of cats	number of legs
1	4
2	
3	
4	
5	
6	

Bugs

number of bugs	number of legs
1	6
2	
3	
4	
5	
6	

Octopuses

number of octopuses	number of legs
1	8
2	
3	
4	
5	
6	

1. How many legs would 6 birds have? _____

2. How many legs would 5 cats have? _____

3. How many legs would 4 bugs have? _____

4. How many legs would 6 octopuses have? _____

5. How many legs would 2 birds and 3 cats have? _____

6. How many legs would 3 cats and 4 bugs have? _____

7. How many legs would 4 birds and 2 octopuses have? _____

8. How many legs would 2 bugs and 3 octopuses have? _____

9. Which has more legs?

    3 birds or 3 cats? _____

    3 birds or 2 bugs? _____

    6 cats or 5 bugs? _____

    2 octopuses or 3 cats? _____

Name _____   Date _____

Smelly Jellies

Directions:

Smelly Jellies are jelly beans that are sold by the bag. Complete the chart for each flavor of Smelly Jellies. Then, use the charts to answer the questions below.

Rotten Egg

number of bags	cost per bag
1	10¢
2	
3	
4	
5	
6	

Skunk

number of bags	cost per bag
1	15¢
2	
3	
4	
5	
6	

Moldy Berry

number of bags	cost per bag
1	20¢
2	
3	
4	
5	
6	

Sour Milk

number of bags	cost per bag
1	25¢
2	
3	
4	
5	
6	

1. How much would 4 bags of Rotten Egg Jellies cost? _____

2. How much would 4 bags of Skunk Jellies cost? _____

3. How much would 4 bags of Moldy Berry Jellies cost? _____

4. How much would 4 bags of Sour Milk Jellies cost? _____

5. How much would 2 bags of each kind cost in all? _____

6. How much would 3 bags of each kind cost in all? _____

7. How much would 5 bags of each kind cost in all? _____

8. How much would 6 bags of each kind cost in all? _____

9. Which costs more? (Circle the answers.)

   5 bags of Rotten Egg Jellies or 5 bags of Moldy Berry Jellies?

   4 bags of Rotten Egg Jellies or 3 bags of Skunk Jellies?

   3 bags of Skunk Jellies or 2 bags of Moldy Berry Jellies?

   6 bags of Moldy Berry Jellies or 5 bags of Sour Milk Jellies?

Name _____ Date _____

Freaky Features

Directions:

Each Xerk has 4 eyes and 2 teeth. Use the picture of 6 Xerks to help you complete the table about Xerks. Then, use the table to answer the questions below.

Number of Xerks	1	2	3	4	5	6	7	8	9	10	11
Number of Eyes	4										
Number of Teeth	2										

1. How many eyes do 5 Xerks have? _____

2. How many teeth do 9 Xerks have? _____

3. How many Xerks will it take to have 28 eyes? _____

4. How many Xerks will it take to have 16 teeth? _____

5. How many eyes and teeth together will 6 Xerks have?

      _____ eyes + _____ teeth = _____ eyes and teeth

6. How many eyes and teeth together will 10 Xerks have?

      _____ eyes + _____ teeth = _____ eyes and teeth

7. Some Xerks got together and counted their eyes and teeth. The total was 30 eyes and teeth.

    How many Xerks were there? _____

8. Some other Xerks got together and counted their eyes and teeth. The total was 66 eyes and teeth.

    How many Xerks were there? _____

Name _____   Date _____

Even Freakier Features   Functions

Directions:
Each Freep has 3 eyes, 4 horns, and 5 teeth. Use the picture of 6 Freeps to help you complete the table about Freeps. Then, use the table to answer the questions below.

Number of Freeps	1	2	3	4	5	6	7	8	9	10	11
Number of Eyes											
Number of Horns											
Number of Teeth											

1. How many eyes do 5 Freeps have? _____

2. How many horns do 8 Freeps have? _____

3. How many teeth do 10 Freeps have? _____

4. How many Freeps will it take to have 21 eyes? _____

5. How many Freeps will it take to have 36 horns? _____

6. How many Freeps will it take to have 35 teeth? _____

7. How many eyes, horns, and teeth together will 5 Freeps have?

   _____ eyes + _____ horns + _____ teeth = _____ eyes, horns, and teeth

8. Some Freeps got together and counted their eyes, horns, and teeth. The total was 36 eyes, horns, and teeth. How many Freeps were there? _____

9. Some other Freeps got together and counted their eyes, horns, and teeth. The total was 96 eyes, horns, and teeth. How many Freeps were there? _____

Dinosaur Minis

Functions

Directions:

The Dino-Mite Plastics Company sells miniature dinosaur figures. Stegosauruses are 2 for 50¢. Tyrannosauruses are 2 for 75¢. Triceratops are 2 for $1.00 (100¢). Complete the charts and use them to answer the questions below.

Stegosaurus

number of dinosaurs	cost (¢)
2	50
4	
6	
8	
10	
12	

Tyrannosaurus

number of dinosaurs	cost (¢)
2	75
4	
6	
8	
10	
12	

Triceratops

number of dinosaurs	cost (¢)
2	100
4	
6	
8	
10	
12	

1. How much would 2 stegosauruses and 2 tyrannosauruses cost together? _____

2. How much would 4 stegosauruses and 6 triceratops cost together? _____

3. How much would 4 tyrannosauruses and 6 triceratops cost together? _____

4. Which costs more?

   4 stegosauruses or 4 tyrannosauruses? _____

   8 stegosauruses or 6 triceratops? _____

5. Which costs less?

   6 tyrannosauruses or 6 triceratops? _____

   10 stegosauruses or 8 triceratops? _____

6. How much would 8 stegosauruses, 8 tyrannosauruses, and 6 triceratops cost in all? _____

Change-O-Matic Machines

Functions

Directions:
Each machine changes a number into another number. Write the number it will be changed into.

Example: 70 |▷ +25 | 95

1. 25 |▷ +25 |

2. 50 |▷ −10 |

3. 15 |▷ +50 |

4. 50 |▷ −25 |

5. 30 |▷ +70 |

6. 100 |▷ −15 |

7. 99 |▷ +10 |

8. 60 |▷ −35 |

9.
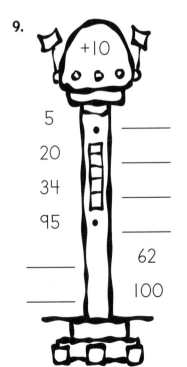

+10

5 _____
20 _____
34 _____
95 _____

_____ 62
_____ 100

10.
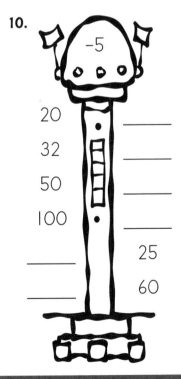

−5

20 _____
32 _____
50 _____
100 _____

_____ 25
_____ 60

11.
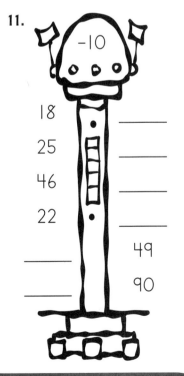

−10

18 _____
25 _____
46 _____
22 _____

_____ 49
_____ 90

More Change-O-Matic Machines

Functions

Directions:

Each machine changes a number into another number. Write the number it will be changed into.

Example: 3 →| x2 |→ 6

1. 6 →| x1 |→

2. 10 →| ÷2 |→

3. 4 →| x5 |→

4. 12 →| ÷3 |→

5. 7 →| x10 |→

6. 20 →| ÷4 |→

7. 5 →| x4 |→

8. 35 →| ÷5 |→

9.
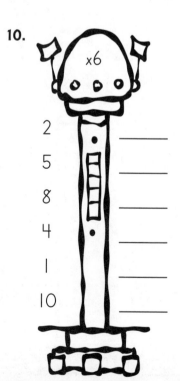

x2

1 ____
2 ____
3 ____
4 ____
5 ____
6 ____

10.

x6

2 ____
5 ____
8 ____
4 ____
1 ____
10 ____

11.
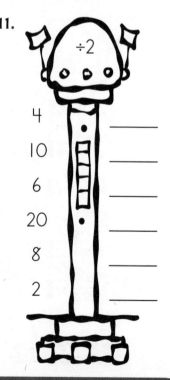

÷2

4 ____
10 ____
6 ____
20 ____
8 ____
2 ____

Double Machines

Functions

Directions:
Each number was put through a Change-O-Matic machine. Then, the number it changed into was put through a second machine. Write the numbers it will change into.

Example: 3 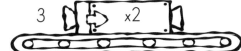 ×2   6 +7 13

1. 10  +4   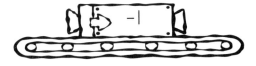 −1

2. 20  −3   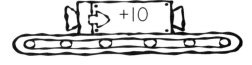 +10

3. 2  +3   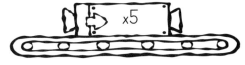 ×5

4. 3  ×4   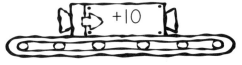 +10

5. 5  −2   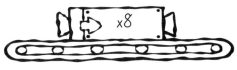 ×8

6. 6  ×5   −3

7. 7  +3   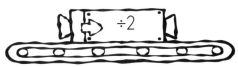 ÷2

8. 20  ÷4   +8

9. 17  −2   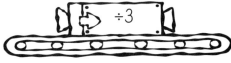 ÷3

10. 3  ×8   ÷6

More Double Machines

Directions:
Each number was put through a Change-O-Matic machine. Then, the number it changed into was put through a second machine. Write the numbers it will be changed into.

1.

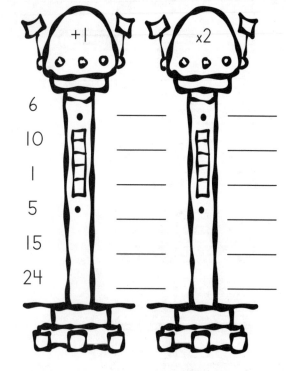

6	___	___
10	___	___
1	___	___
5	___	___
15	___	___
24	___	___

2.

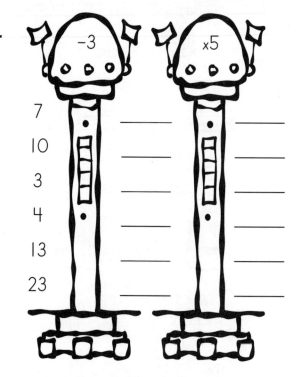

7	___	___
10	___	___
3	___	___
4	___	___
13	___	___
23	___	___

3.

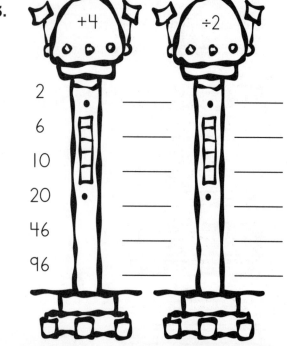

2	___	___
6	___	___
10	___	___
20	___	___
46	___	___
96	___	___

4.

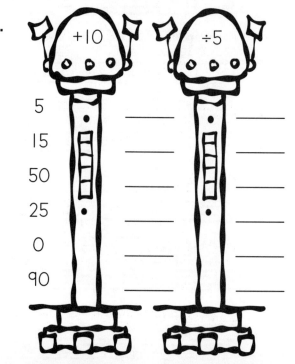

5	___	___
15	___	___
50	___	___
25	___	___
0	___	___
90	___	___

 Elementary Algebra • CD-104105

Missing Programs

Functions

Directions:

Each number was put through a Change-O-Matic machine. Then, the number it changed into was put through a second machine to change it into another number. But, the programs that tell the machines how to change the numbers are missing. Use the numbers 1, 2, or 3 to accurately program the machines and write the numbers the first numbers changed into.

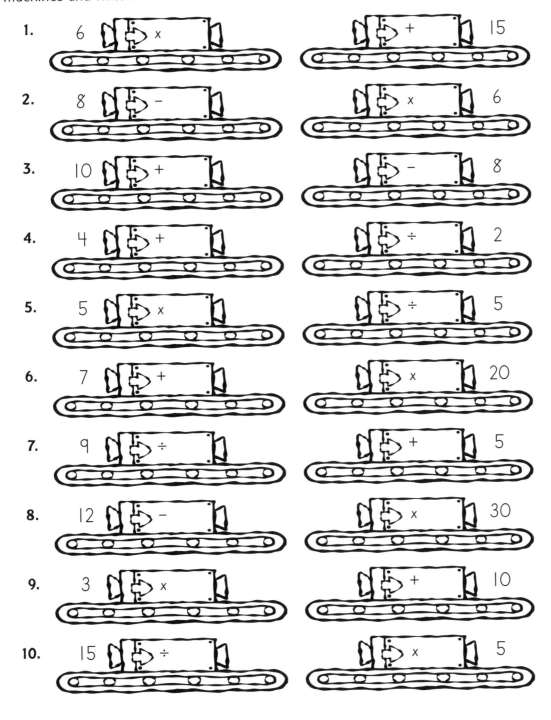

1. 6 [×] [+] 15

2. 8 [−] [×] 6

3. 10 [+] [−] 8

4. 4 [+] [÷] 2

5. 5 [×] [÷] 5

6. 7 [+] [×] 20

7. 9 [÷] [+] 5

8. 12 [−] [×] 30

9. 3 [×] [+] 10

10. 15 [÷] [×] 5

Name _____ Date _____

Equal or Not Equal?

Directions:

Some kids were comparing their jelly beans. Write a number sentence for each situation to tell whether the amount of the kids' jelly beans are equal or not equal.

Example:

Kyle has 10 red jelly beans.
Patsy has 5 red jelly beans
and 6 blue ones.

$$10 \neq 5 + 6$$

1. Anna has 6 yellow jelly beans
   and 3 orange ones.
   Bella has 9 pink jelly beans.

   _____

2. Chas has 12 purple jelly beans.
   Oscar has 6 green jelly beans
   and 5 blue ones.

   _____

3. Ernie has 7 red jelly beans
   and 9 black ones.
   Fritz has 15 white jelly beans.

   _____

4. Forrest has 13 blue jelly beans.
   Dixon has 6 yellow jelly beans
   and 7 purple ones.

   _____

5. Iggie has 9 orange jelly beans
   and 8 pink ones.
   Sharelle has 17 black jelly beans.

   _____

6. Kiko has 19 white jelly beans.
   Loren has 8 green jelly beans
   and 10 blue ones.

   _____

7. Micah has 13 red jelly beans
   and 12 pink ones.
   Nina has 25 yellow jelly beans.

   _____

Comparing Kitty Treats

Directions:

Some pet owners were comparing the number of cheese and fish treats they gave to their cats. Write a number sentence for each comparison to show if the number of treats are equal or not equal.

Example: Frisky   Tiger

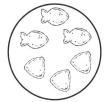 

3 + 3 = 2 + 4

1.   Mittens   Socks

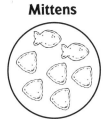

_____

2.   Itsy   Bitsy

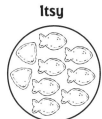 

_____

3.   Fuzzy   Wuzzy

 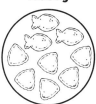

_____

4.   Foxy   Roxy

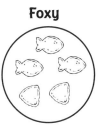 

_____

5.   Robin   Jay

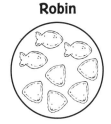 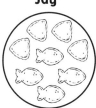

_____

6.   Cocoa   Coffee

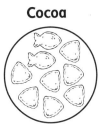 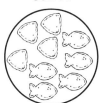

_____

7.   Flash   Crash

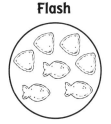 

_____

Chocolate Chip Math

Directions:

Draw more chocolate chips on one cookie in each box to make the sets equal. Write a number sentence to show what you did.

Example:

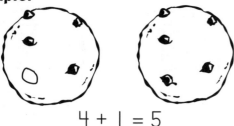

$4 + 1 = 5$

1.

_____

2.

_____

3.

_____

4.

_____

5.

_____

6.

_____

7.

_____

Comparing Doggy Treats

Equality

Directions:
Some pet owners were totaling the number of bone and cheese treats they gave to their dogs. Circle the sentences that are true about each picture.

1.	Randy	Jasper

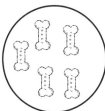 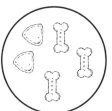

Randy	Jasper
5 = 3 + 2	4 + 1 = 5
3 + 2 = 6	3 = 2 + 5
5 = 2 + 3	2 + 3 = 5

2.	Barker	Lucky

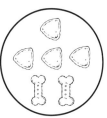 

Barker	Lucky
4 + 2 = 6	6 + 4 = 2
4 + 2 = 7	6 = 2 + 4
6 = 3 + 3	6 = 4 + 2

3.	Peanut	Rover

 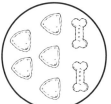

Peanut	Rover
7 + 2 = 5	7 = 2 + 5
7 = 5 + 2	5 = 2 + 7
7 = 2 + 4	2 + 5 = 7

4.	Tiger	Spot

 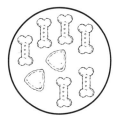 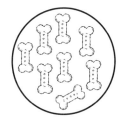

Tiger	Spot
6 + 8 = 2	6 + 2 = 8
8 = 6 + 3	2 + 6 = 8
8 = 2 + 6	6 = 2 + 8

5.	Buddy	Goofy

Buddy	Goofy
9 = 4 + 5	9 + 4 = 5
5 + 4 = 9	9 = 5 + 4
4 = 9 + 5	9 = 6 + 2

6.	Max	Kane

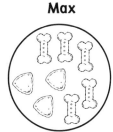 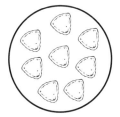

Max	Kane
3 + 8 = 5	3 + 5 = 8
8 = 5 + 3	3 = 8 + 5
8 = 3 + 4	8 = 3 + 5

Name _____   Date _____

Munching Math

Equality

Directions:

There are two sets of brownies in each box. Make the sets equal by "munching" some brownies. Cross out the brownies and write a number sentence to show how you made the sets equal.

Example: 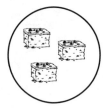 $4 - 1 = 3$	**1.**  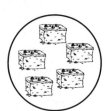 _____
2. 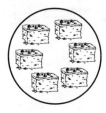 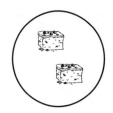 _____	**3.** 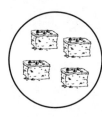 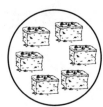 _____
4. 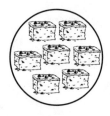 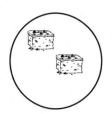 _____	**5.** 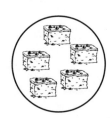 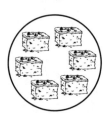 _____
6. 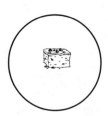  _____	**7.** 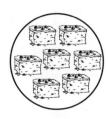 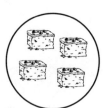 _____

Name _____   Date _____

Balancing Act   **Equality**

Directions:
Look at the numbers on the ends of each balance. Should they stay balanced? Circle yes or no.

1.
   6   4 + 2
   yes   no

2.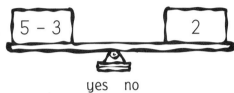
   5 − 3   2
   yes   no

3.
   4 + 3   8
   yes   no

4.
   4   10 − 6
   yes   no

5.
   10 + 10   19
   yes   no

6.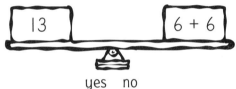
   13   6 + 6
   yes   no

7.
   12   16 − 4
   yes   no

8.
   15 − 6   9
   yes   no

9.
   3 + 4   4 + 4
   yes   no

10.
    8 + 6   6 + 8
    yes   no

11.
    9 − 6   2 + 1
    yes   no

12.
    8 − 4   10 − 6
    yes   no

13.
    6 − 4   7 − 4
    yes   no

14.
    6 + 2   9 − 1
    yes   no

Balancing Act 2

Equality

Directions:

Look at the numbers on the ends of each balance. Should they stay balanced? Circle yes or no.

1.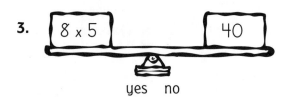
   yes   no

2.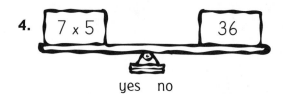
   yes   no

3.
   yes   no

4.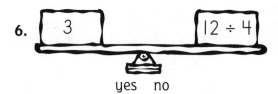
   yes   no

5.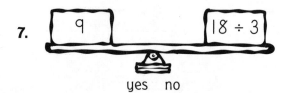
   yes   no

6.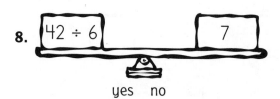
   yes   no

7.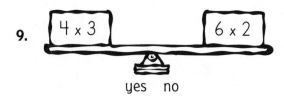
   yes   no

8.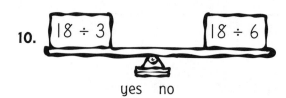
   yes   no

9.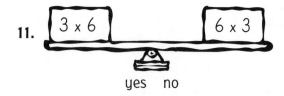
   yes   no

10.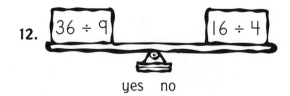
    yes   no

11.
    yes   no

12.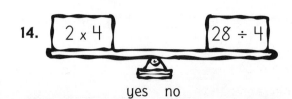
    yes   no

13. 50 ÷ 5   5 x 2
    yes   no

14. 2 x 4   28 ÷ 4
    yes   no

Name _____   Date _____

Card Collections

Differences

Directions:

Twins Kate and Nate collect cards. Answer the questions below about their collections.

1.   **Soccer Cards**

Kate

Nate

Who has more?_____

How many more? _____

Who has less?_____

How many less? _____

2.   **Tennis Cards**

Kate

Nate

Who has more? _____

How many more? _____

Who has less? _____

How many less? _____

3.   **Golf Cards**

Kate

Nate

Who has more?_____

How many more? _____

Who has less?_____

How many less? _____

4.   **Volleyball Cards**

Kate

Nate

Who has more? _____

How many more? _____

Who has less? _____

How many less? _____

5.   **Hockey Cards**

Kate has 15 cards.

Nate has 20 cards.

Who has more?_____

How many more? _____

Who has less?_____

How many less? _____

6.   **Baseball Cards**

Kate has 40 cards.

Nate has 25 cards.

Who has more? _____

How many more? _____

Who has less? _____

How many less? _____

7.   **Football Cards**

Kate has 50 cards.

Nate has 25 cards.

Who has more?_____

How many more? _____

Who has less?_____

How many less? _____

8.   **Basketball Cards**

Kate has 110 cards.

Nate has 154 cards.

Who has more? _____

How many more? _____

Who has less? _____

How many less? _____

More Card Collections

Directions:

Twins Kate and Nate collect Olympic cards, too. Shade the squares to show how many cards they each have. Then, answer the questions about their collections

1.   **Cycling Cards**

Kate

Nate

Kate has 7 cards.

Nate has 3 more.

How many cards does Nate have? _____

2.   **Diving Cards**

Kate

Nate

Nate has 8 cards.

Kate has 2 more.

How many cards does Kate have? _____

3.   **Canoeing Cards**

Kate

Nate

Kate has 10 cards.

Nate has 4 less.

How many cards does Nate have? _____

4.   **Wrestling Cards**

Kate

Nate

Nate has 9 cards.

Kate has 1 less.

How many cards does Kate have? _____

5.   **Swimming Cards**

Kate has 35 cards.

Nate has 15 more.

How many cards does Nate have? _____

6.   **Gymnastics Cards**

Nate has 47 cards.

Kate has 25 more.

How many cards does Kate have? _____

7.   **Volleyball Cards**

Kate has 122 cards.

Nate has 28 less.

How many cards does Nate have? _____

8.   **Equestrian Cards**

Nate has 135 cards.

Kate has 17 less.

How many cards does Kate have? _____

Name _____   Date _____

Tropical Fish

 Differences

Directions:

Figure out the difference between the number of each type of fish Gina and Kay have. Then, write an addition sentence and a subtraction sentence about the difference. Circle the difference.

Neon Tetras

Example: Difference is __2__.

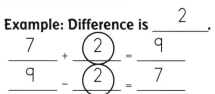

Angelfish

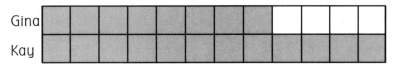

1. Difference is _____.

_____ + _____ = _____

_____ − _____ = _____

Swordtails

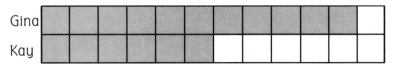

2. Difference is _____.

_____ + _____ = _____

_____ − _____ = _____

Giant Danios

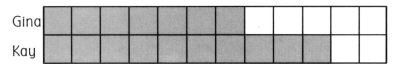

3. Difference is _____.

_____ + _____ = _____

_____ − _____ = _____

Moonfish

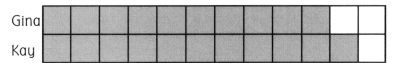

4. Difference is _____.

_____ + _____ = _____

_____ − _____ = _____

Jewelfish

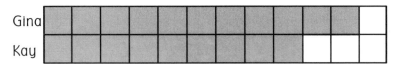

5. Difference is _____.

_____ + _____ = _____

_____ − _____ = _____

Clown Barbs

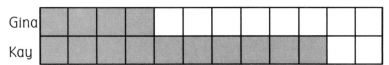

6. Difference is _____.

_____ + _____ = _____

_____ − _____ = _____

 Elementary Algebra • CD-104105

Name _____   Date _____

Making Pizzas

Differences

Directions:

Dan and his brother Randy made their own pizzas. Write a number sentence about each problem. Put a blank line (___) in the sentence to show what is not known. Then, solve the problem.

Example:

Dan used 11 pieces of bacon on his pizza. That is 2 more than Randy used. How many pieces of bacon did Randy use?

sentence: $11 = \underline{} + 2$

___9___ pieces of bacon

1. Dan used 15 pieces of green pepper on his pizza. That is 2 less than Randy used. How many pieces of green pepper did Randy use?

sentence: _____

_____ pieces of green pepper

2. Randy used 12 onion slices on his pizza. That is 3 more than Dan used. How many onion slices did Dan use?

sentence: _____

_____ onion slices

3. Randy used 21 pieces of cheese on his pizza. That is 10 less than Dan used. How many pieces of cheese did Dan use?

sentence: _____

_____ pieces of cheese

4. Dan used 19 tomato chunks on his pizza. That is 4 less than Randy used. How many tomato chunks did Randy use?

sentence: _____

_____ tomato chunks

5. Dan used 30 pepperoni slices on his pizza. That is 9 more than Randy used. How many pepperoni slices did Randy use?

sentence: _____

_____ pepperoni slices

6. Randy used 14 mushrooms on his pizza. That is 14 more than Dan used. How many mushrooms did Dan use?

sentence: _____

_____ mushrooms

7. Randy used 15 pieces of ham on his pizza. That is 8 less than Dan used. How many pieces of ham did Dan use?

sentence: _____

_____ pieces of ham

Name _____   Date _____

Trodo the Troll

Directions:
Trodo the Troll had a lot of interesting collections. He decided to sort them. Write a multiplication sentence about each of his collections.

Example:

Trodo collected puff balls.
He put them in 7 containers.
He put 5 in each container.
He had 35 puff balls.

$$\underline{\quad 7 \times 5 = 35 \quad}$$

1. Trodo collected shiny rocks.
He put them in 8 bags.
He put 6 in each bag.
He had 48 shiny rocks.

_____

2. Trodo collected pieces of moss.
He arranged them in 6 stacks.
He put 7 in each stack.
He had 42 pieces of moss.

_____

3. Trodo collected pinecones.
He put them in 4 cans.
He put 9 in each can.
He had 36 pinecones.

_____

4. Trodo collected dried mushrooms.
He put them in 5 jars.
He put 11 in each jar.
He had 55 dried mushrooms.

_____

5. Trodo collected sticks.
He put them in 12 bags.
He put 7 in each bag.
He had 84 sticks.

_____

6. Trodo collected poison ivy leaves.
He put them in 10 jars.
He put 13 in each jar.
He had 130 poison ivy leaves.

_____

7. Trodo collected bird eggshells.
He put them in 8 old egg cartons.
He put 12 in each carton.
He had 96 bird eggshells.

_____

Name _____   Date _____

Party Candy

Directions:

Zelda and her friends sorted the candy they got at her birthday party. Write a division sentence about each type of candy.

Example:

They had 28 candy bars.
They put them in 7 bags.
They put 4 in each bag.

$$28 \div 7 = 4$$

1. They had 40 pieces of taffy.
   They put them in 5 bags.
   They put 8 in each bag.

   _____

2. They had 64 hard fruit candies.
   They put them in 8 bags.
   They put 8 in each bag.

   _____

3. They had 54 wax lips.
   They put them in 6 bags.
   They put 9 in each bag.

   _____

4. They had 36 packs of gum.
   They put them in 3 bags.
   They put 12 in each bag.

   _____

5. They had 50 peanut butter cups.
   They put them in 10 bags.
   They put 5 in each bag.

   _____

6. They had 90 gummy creatures.
   They put them in 6 bags.
   They put 15 in each bag.

   _____

7. They had 100 caramels.
   They put them in 4 bags.
   They put 25 in each bag.

   _____

Name _____   Date _____

Operation Cleanup

Directions:
Kiki had to clean her room. Write a number sentence about each story. You may use +, −, x, or ÷.

1. Kiki had 13 baseball caps;
   7 were red and 6 were
   blue. She hung up all of them.

   _____

2. Kiki had 25 toy ponies.
   She put 15 in her closet
   and kept 10 on her display shelf.

   _____

3. Kiki put her magazines in
   3 stacks. There were 8 in each
   stack. She had 24 magazines
   in all.

   _____

4. Kiki had 18 fashion dolls.
   She put 6 dolls in each drawer.
   She used 3 drawers.

   _____

5. Kiki had 35 barrettes. She
   arranged them in her drawer
   in 5 rows with 7 barrettes
   in each row.

   _____

6. Kiki had 15 glitter bouncy balls
   and 25 solid bouncy balls.
   Altogether she had 40 bouncy
   balls. She put them in a box.

   _____

7. Kiki had 4 sets of animal books
   with 6 books in each set. She put
   all 24 animal books on the shelf.

   _____

8. Kiki had 12 model planes. She
   put away the 4 that were glued
   together and kept the other 8 out.

   _____

Name _____   Date _____

Videos and CDs

Directions:
Read the story in each box. Then, draw a picture and write a number sentence with a blank space (___)
in it to show what is not known. Solve each number sentence.

1. Fawn has 7 CDs and 8 videos. How many is that altogether? sentence: _____ _____ CDs and videos	**2.** Robin had 6 cartoon videos. Her friend had 10 cartoon videos. How many more should Robin get if she wants to have the same number of cartoon videos as her friend? sentence: _____ _____ cartoon videos
3. Kat had 12 music CDs. She gave her brother 3 of them. How many music CDs does she have now? sentence: _____ _____ music CDs	**4.** Teddy had 15 videos. He lost some. Now, he has 9. How many did he lose? sentence: _____ _____ videos
5. Shenille had some rock CDs. She got 4 more. Now, she has 13. How many rock CDs did she have to begin with? sentence: _____ _____ rock CDs	**6.** Darrell had some videos. He broke 6 of them. Now, he has 5 left. How many did he have to begin with? sentence: _____ _____ videos

Name _____   Date _____

Directions:

Read the story in each box. Then, draw a picture and write a number sentence with a blank space (____) in it to show what is not known. Solve each number sentence.

---

1. Bert has 3 sets of square blocks. There are 9 square blocks in each set. How many square blocks does Bert have?

sentence: _____

_____ square blocks

---

2. Bert has 32 plastic blocks. He put them in stacks of 4. How many stacks could he make?

sentence: _____

_____ stacks

---

3. Bert has 4 sets of triangular blocks. There are 12 in each set. How many triangular blocks does he have now?

sentence: _____

_____ triangular blocks

---

4. Bert has 30 animal blocks. He put the same number in each bag. He used 6 bags. How many animals blocks did he put in each bag?

sentence: _____

_____ animal blocks

---

5. Bert has 35 hexagonal blocks. He put them in sets of 7. How many sets did he make?

sentence: _____

_____ sets

---

6. Bert has some log blocks. He put them in 3 piles. He put 12 in each pile. How many log blocks does he have?

sentence: _____

_____ log blocks

Name _____   Date _____

Write Your Own Math Stories

Directions:
Write a math story to go with each number sentence below.

Example:
16 + 15 = 31   I had 16 rocks. Then, I found 15 more on a hike. Now, I have 31 rocks.

1. 35 – 14 = 21   _____

_____

_____

_____

2. 8 + 7 = 15   _____

_____

_____

_____

3. 6 x 5 = 30   _____

_____

_____

_____

4. 24 ÷ 6 = 4   _____

_____

_____

_____

5. 9 x 10 = 90   _____

_____

_____

_____

Write Your Own Sentences

Directions:

Fill in the blanks to make true number sentences. Do not use 0 or 1. Make each sentence different.

1. _____ + _____ = _____

2. _____ - _____ = _____

3. _____ = _____ + _____

4. _____ = _____ - _____

5. _____ + _____ = _____

6. _____ - _____ = _____

7. _____ = _____ + _____

8. _____ = _____ - _____

9. _____ + _____ = _____

10. _____ - _____ = _____

11. _____ = _____ + _____

12. _____ = _____ - _____

13. _____ + _____ = _____

14. _____ - _____ = _____

15. _____ = _____ + _____

16. _____ = _____ - _____

17. _____ + _____ = _____

18. _____ - _____ = _____

19. _____ = _____ + _____

20. _____ = _____ - _____

21. _____ + _____ = _____

22. _____ - _____ = _____

23. _____ = _____ + _____

24. _____ = _____ - _____

25. _____ + _____ = _____

26. _____ - _____ = _____

27. _____ = _____ + _____

28. _____ = _____ - _____

Addition Sentences

Directions:
Write more addition sentences in each box. Use a pattern to help you.

1. **Sentences about 10**	**2.** **Sentences about 12**
$10 = 0 + 10$	$12 = 0 + 12$
$10 = 1 + 9$	$12 = 1 + 11$
$10 = 2 + 8$	$12 = 2 + 10$
$10 = $ _____	$12 = $ _____
$10 = $ _____	$12 = $ _____
$10 = $ _____	$12 = $ _____
$10 = $ _____	$12 = $ _____
$10 = $ _____	$12 = $ _____
$10 = $ _____	$12 = $ _____
3. **Sentences about 15**	**4.** **Sentences about 20**
$15 = 0 + 15$	$20 = 0 + 20$
$15 = 1 + 14$	$20 = 1 + 19$
$15 = $ _____	$20 = $ _____
$15 = $ _____	$20 = $ _____
$15 = $ _____	$20 = $ _____
$15 = $ _____	$20 = $ _____
$15 = $ _____	$20 = $ _____
$15 = $ _____	$20 = $ _____
$15 = $ _____	$20 = $ _____
$15 = $ _____	$20 = $ _____

Subtraction Sentences

Directions:

Write more subtraction sentences in each box. Use a pattern to help you.

1.	Sentences about 2

$2 = 2 - 0$

$2 = 3 - 1$

$2 = 4 - 2$

$2 =$ _____

$2 =$ _____

$2 =$ _____

$2 =$ _____

$2 =$ _____

$2 =$ _____

2.	Sentences about 3

$3 = 3 - 0$

$3 = 4 - 1$

$3 = 5 - 2$

$3 =$ _____

$3 =$ _____

$3 =$ _____

$3 =$ _____

$3 =$ _____

$3 =$ _____

3.	Sentences about 4

$4 = 4 - 0$

$4 = 5 - 1$

$4 =$ _____

$4 =$ _____

$4 =$ _____

$4 =$ _____

$4 =$ _____

$4 =$ _____

$4 =$ _____

4.	Sentences about 5

$5 = 5 - 0$

$5 = 6 - 1$

$5 =$ _____

$5 =$ _____

$5 =$ _____

$5 =$ _____

$5 =$ _____

$5 =$ _____

$5 =$ _____

Number Families

Directions:
Each set of numbers belongs to a family. Write 8 addition and subtraction sentences about each family.

1. **Family of 6, 3, and 9**

$6 + 3 = 9$

$9 = 6 + 3$

___ + ___ = ___

___ = ___ + ___

$9 - 6 = 3$

$3 = 9 - 6$

___ - ___ = ___

___ = ___ - ___

2. **Family of 7, 2, and 5**

3. **Family of 8, 5, and 3**

4. **Family of 6, 0, and 6**

Fill in the Blanks

Writing Number Sentences

Directions:
Fill in the blanks to make each sentence true. Do not use 0 or 1.

1. $3 + $ _____ $= $ _____

2. _____ $= 6 + $ _____

3. _____ $+ 8 = $ _____

4. _____ $= $ _____ $+ 4$

5. _____ $+ $ _____ $= 5$

6. $7 = $ _____ $+ $ _____

7. $7 - $ _____ $= $ _____

8. _____ $= 10 - $ _____

9. _____ $- 3 = $ _____

10. _____ $= $ _____ $- 5$

11. _____ $- $ _____ $= 4$

12. $6 = $ _____ $- $ _____

13. _____ $+ 7 = $ _____

14. _____ $= $ _____ $+ 5$

15. $5 + $ _____ $= $ _____

16. _____ $= 10 + $ _____

17. $8 - $ _____ $= $ _____

18. _____ $= 12 - $ _____

19. _____ $- $ _____ $= 9$

20. $8 = $ _____ $- $ _____

21. _____ $+ $ _____ $+ $ _____ $= 15$

22. _____ $+ $ _____ $+ $ _____ $+ $ _____ $= 20$

23. _____ $+ $ _____ $+ $ _____ $+ $ _____ $+ $ _____ $= 100$

Write Your Own

Directions:

Fill in the blanks to make true multiplication sentences. Do not use 0 or 1. Make each sentence different.

1. _____ x _____ = _____

2. _____ = _____ x _____

3. _____ x _____ = _____

4. _____ = _____ x _____

5. _____ x _____ = _____

6. _____ = _____ x _____

7. _____ x _____ = _____

8. _____ = _____ x _____

9. _____ x _____ = _____

10. _____ = _____ x _____

11. _____ x _____ = _____

12. _____ = _____ x _____

13. _____ x _____ = _____

14. _____ = _____ x _____

15. _____ x _____ = _____

16. _____ = _____ x _____

17. _____ x _____ = _____

18. _____ = _____ x _____

19. _____ x _____ = _____

20. _____ = _____ x _____

21. _____ x _____ = _____

22. _____ = _____ x _____

23. _____ x _____ = _____

24. _____ = _____ x _____

Name _____   Date _____

Fill in the Blanks Again

Directions:

Fill in the blanks to make each sentence true. Do not use 0 or 1.

1. $3 \times$ _____ = _____

2. _____ $= 4 \times$ _____

3. $6 \times$ _____ = _____

4. _____ $= 7 \times$ _____

5. _____ $\times 5 =$ _____

6. _____ $=$ _____ $\times 8$

7. _____ $\times 1 =$ _____

8. _____ $=$ _____ $\times 2$

9. _____ $\times$ _____ $= 12$

10. $20 =$ _____ $\times$ _____

11. _____ $\times$ _____ $= 16$

12. $24 =$ _____ $\times$ _____

13. $9 \times$ _____ = _____

14. _____ $= 10 \times$ _____

15. _____ $\times 8 =$ _____

16. _____ $=$ _____ $\times 1$

17. _____ $\times$ _____ $= 18$

18. $21 =$ _____ $\times$ _____

19. $20 \times$ _____ = _____

20. _____ $= 15 \times$ _____

Multiplication Sentences

Directions:

Write multiplication sentences in each box. Use a pattern to help you.

1. Sentences about 16	**2. Sentences about 12**
$16 = 1 \times 16$	$12 = $ _____
$16 = 16 \times 1$	$12 = $ _____
$16 = 2 \times 8$	$12 = $ _____
$16 = $ _____	$12 = $ _____
$16 = $ _____	$12 = $ _____
	$12 = $ _____
3. Sentences about 18	**4. Sentences about 24**
$18 = $ _____	$24 = $ _____
$18 = $ _____	$24 = $ _____
$18 = $ _____	$24 = $ _____
$18 = $ _____	$24 = $ _____
$18 = $ _____	$24 = $ _____
$18 = $ _____	$24 = $ _____
5. Sentences about 30	**6. Sentences about 36**
$30 = $ _____	$36 = $ _____
$30 = $ _____	$36 = $ _____
$30 = $ _____	$36 = $ _____
$30 = $ _____	$36 = $ _____
$30 = $ _____	$36 = $ _____
$30 = $ _____	$36 = $ _____

Write Your Own Again

Directions:

Fill in the blanks to make true division sentences. Do not use 0 or 1. Make each sentence different.

1. _____ ÷ _____ = _____

2. _____ = _____ ÷ _____

3. _____ ÷ _____ = _____

4. _____ = _____ ÷ _____

5. _____ ÷ _____ = _____

6. _____ = _____ ÷ _____

7. _____ ÷ _____ = _____

8. _____ = _____ ÷ _____

9. _____ ÷ _____ = _____

10. _____ = _____ ÷ _____

11. _____ ÷ _____ = _____

12. _____ = _____ ÷ _____

13. _____ ÷ _____ = _____

14. _____ = _____ ÷ _____

15. _____ ÷ _____ = _____

16. _____ = _____ ÷ _____

17. _____ ÷ _____ = _____

18. _____ = _____ ÷ _____

19. _____ ÷ _____ = _____

20. _____ = _____ ÷ _____

21. _____ ÷ _____ = _____

22. _____ = _____ ÷ _____

23. _____ ÷ _____ = _____

24. _____ = _____ ÷ _____

Name _____ Date _____

Fill in the Blanks One More Time

Directions:
Fill in the blanks to make each sentence true. Do not use 0 or 1.

1. _____ ÷ 3 = _____

2. _____ = _____ ÷ 5

3. _____ ÷ 2 = _____

4. _____ = _____ ÷ 4

5. _____ ÷ _____ = 1

6. 2 = _____ ÷ _____

7. _____ ÷ _____ = 6

8. 4 = _____ ÷ _____

9. 12 ÷ _____ = _____

10. _____ = 10 ÷ _____

11. 15 ÷ _____ = _____

12. _____ = 30 ÷ _____

13. _____ ÷ 7 = _____

14. _____ = _____ ÷ 8

15. _____ ÷ _____ = 3

16. 5 = _____ ÷ _____

17. 25 ÷ _____ = _____

18. _____ = 32 ÷ _____

19. _____ ÷ 10 = _____

20. _____ = _____ ÷ 9

Division Sentences

Directions:
Write division sentences in each box. Use a pattern to help you.

1. Sentences about 2	**2. Sentences about 3**

1. Sentences about 2

$2 = 2 ÷ 1$

$2 = 4 ÷ 2$

$2 = 6 ÷ 3$

$2 = $ _____

$2 = $ _____

$2 = $ _____

$2 = $ _____

$2 = $ _____

$2 = $ _____

$2 = $ _____

2. Sentences about 3

$3 = 3 ÷ 1$

$3 = 6 ÷ 2$

$3 = 9 ÷ 3$

$3 = $ _____

$3 = $ _____

$3 = $ _____

$3 = $ _____

$3 = $ _____

$3 = $ _____

$3 = $ _____

3. Sentences about 4

$4 = 4 ÷ 1$

$4 = 8 ÷ 2$

$4 = $ _____

$4 = $ _____

$4 = $ _____

$4 = $ _____

$4 = $ _____

$4 = $ _____

$4 = $ _____

$4 = $ _____

4. Sentences about 5

$5 = 5 ÷ 1$

$5 = 10 ÷ 2$

$5 = $ _____

$5 = $ _____

$5 = $ _____

$5 = $ _____

$5 = $ _____

$5 = $ _____

$5 = $ _____

$5 = $ _____

Other Number Families

Directions:

Each set of numbers belongs to a family. Write 8 multiplication and division sentences about each family.

1. **Family of 5, 20, and 4**

$5 \times 4 = 20$

$20 = 5 \times 4$

____ $\times$ ____ = ____

____ = ____ $\times$ ____

$20 \div 5 = 4$

$4 = 20 \div 5$

____ $\div$ ____ = ____

____ = ____ $\div$ ____

2. **Family of 6, 3, and 18**

3. **Family of 28, 7, and 4**

4. **Family of 9, 9, and 1**

Watch the Signs

Directions:
Fill in the blanks to make true number sentences. Do not use 0 or 1. Make each sentence different.

1. _____ + _____ = _____

2. _____ = _____ + _____

3. _____ – _____ = _____

4. _____ = _____ – _____

5. _____ x _____ = _____

6. _____ = _____ x _____

7. _____ ÷ _____ = _____

8. _____ = _____ ÷ _____

9. _____ + _____ = _____

10. _____ = _____ + _____

11. _____ – _____ = _____

12. _____ = _____ – _____

13. _____ x _____ = _____

14. _____ = _____ x _____

15. _____ ÷ _____ = _____

16. _____ = _____ ÷ _____

17. _____ + _____ = _____

18. _____ = _____ + _____

19. _____ – _____ = _____

20. _____ = _____ – _____

21. _____ x _____ = _____

22. _____ = _____ x _____

23. _____ ÷ _____ = _____

24. _____ = _____ ÷ _____

Name _____ Date _____

Pizzas with Everything

Directions:
Each number pizza has a little bit of everything on it. Fill in the blanks to make each number sentence true. Do not use 0.

1.
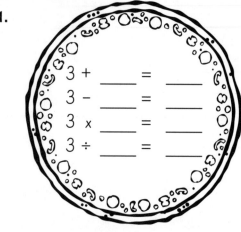

$3 + \underline{\hspace{1cm}} = \underline{\hspace{1cm}}$
$3 - \underline{\hspace{1cm}} = \underline{\hspace{1cm}}$
$3 \times \underline{\hspace{1cm}} = \underline{\hspace{1cm}}$
$3 \div \underline{\hspace{1cm}} = \underline{\hspace{1cm}}$

2.

$\underline{\hspace{1cm}} = 6 + \underline{\hspace{1cm}}$
$\underline{\hspace{1cm}} = 6 - \underline{\hspace{1cm}}$
$\underline{\hspace{1cm}} = 6 \times \underline{\hspace{1cm}}$
$\underline{\hspace{1cm}} = 6 \div \underline{\hspace{1cm}}$

3.
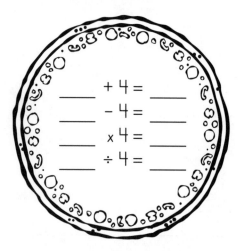

$\underline{\hspace{1cm}} + 4 = \underline{\hspace{1cm}}$
$\underline{\hspace{1cm}} - 4 = \underline{\hspace{1cm}}$
$\underline{\hspace{1cm}} \times 4 = \underline{\hspace{1cm}}$
$\underline{\hspace{1cm}} \div 4 = \underline{\hspace{1cm}}$

4.
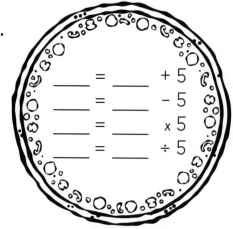

$\underline{\hspace{1cm}} = \underline{\hspace{1cm}} + 5$
$\underline{\hspace{1cm}} = \underline{\hspace{1cm}} - 5$
$\underline{\hspace{1cm}} = \underline{\hspace{1cm}} \times 5$
$\underline{\hspace{1cm}} = \underline{\hspace{1cm}} \div 5$

5.
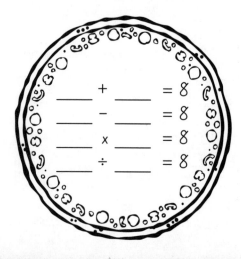

$\underline{\hspace{1cm}} + \underline{\hspace{1cm}} = 8$
$\underline{\hspace{1cm}} - \underline{\hspace{1cm}} = 8$
$\underline{\hspace{1cm}} \times \underline{\hspace{1cm}} = 8$
$\underline{\hspace{1cm}} \div \underline{\hspace{1cm}} = 8$

6.

$12 = \underline{\hspace{1cm}} + \underline{\hspace{1cm}}$
$12 = \underline{\hspace{1cm}} - \underline{\hspace{1cm}}$
$12 = \underline{\hspace{1cm}} \times \underline{\hspace{1cm}}$
$12 = \underline{\hspace{1cm}} \div \underline{\hspace{1cm}}$

Hidden Number Sentences

Directions:

In each box, find the three numbers that will complete a number sentence. Complete the number sentence and shade the three boxes.

1.

7	2	3
11	6	10

___ + ___ = ___

2.

12	8	11
2	7	6

___ − ___ = ___

3.

12	5	6
3	14	4

___ x ___ = ___

4.

5	18	9
21	3	6

___ ÷ ___ = ___

5.

7	13	8
12	4	2

___ + ___ = ___

6.

13	5	6
14	4	7

___ − ___ = ___

7.

7	24	4
20	6	8

___ = ___ x ___

8.

25	5	6
3	4	15

___ = ___ ÷ ___

9.

9	14	8
2	1	4

___ = ___ + ___

10.

11	4	16
2	10	8

___ = ___ − ___

11.

6	2	9
18	4	27

___ = ___ x ___

12.

15	12	8
4	2	5

___ = ___ ÷ ___

Both Sides

Directions:

Fill in the blanks to make true number sentences. Do not repeat one side of the equal sign on the other side. Make each sentence different. Do not use 0 or 1.

1. _____ + _____ = _____ + _____

2. _____ + _____ = _____ + _____

3. _____ + _____ = _____ + _____

4. _____ + _____ = _____ + _____

5. _____ – _____ = _____ – _____

6. _____ – _____ = _____ – _____

7. _____ – _____ = _____ – _____

8. _____ – _____ = _____ – _____

9. _____ + _____ = _____ – _____

10. _____ – _____ = _____ + _____

11. _____ + _____ = _____ – _____

12. _____ – _____ = _____ + _____

13. _____ + _____ = _____ + _____

14. _____ – _____ = _____ + _____

Both Sides Again

Directions:
Fill in the blanks to make true number sentences. Do not repeat one side of the equal sign on the other side. Make each sentence different. Do not use 0 or 1.

1. _____ x _____ = _____ x _____

2. _____ x _____ = _____ x _____

3. _____ ÷ _____ = _____ ÷ _____

4. _____ ÷ _____ = _____ ÷ _____

5. _____ + _____ = _____ x _____

6. _____ x _____ = _____ + _____

7. _____ − _____ = _____ x _____

8. _____ x _____ = _____ − _____

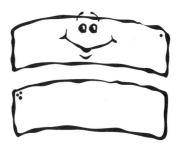

9. _____ + _____ = _____ ÷ _____

10. _____ ÷ _____ = _____ + _____

11. _____ − _____ = _____ ÷ _____

12. _____ ÷ _____ = _____ − _____

13. _____ x _____ = _____ ÷ _____

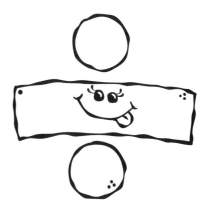

14. _____ ÷ _____ = _____ x _____

Double Your Brain Power!

Directions:

Answer the doubles problems. Then, use doubles to help you solve other problems.

1. $1 + 1 =$ _____

2. $2 + 2 =$ _____

3. $3 + 3 =$ _____

4. $4 + 4 =$ _____

5. $5 + 5 =$ _____

6. $6 + 6 =$ _____

7. $7 + 7 =$ _____

8. $8 + 8 =$ _____

9. $9 + 9 =$ _____

10. $10 + 10 =$ _____

11. $11 + 11 =$ _____

12. $12 + 12 =$ _____

13. $13 + 13 =$ _____

14. $14 + 14 =$ _____

15. $15 + 15 =$ _____

16. $2 + 2 = 4$ so $2 + 3 =$ _____

17. $3 + 3 = 6$ so $3 + 4 =$ _____

18. $4 + 4 = 8$ so $4 + 5 =$ _____

19. $5 + 5 = 10$ so $5 + 6 =$ _____

20. $6 + 6 = 12$ so $6 + 7 =$ _____

21. $7 + 7 = 14$ so $7 + 8 =$ _____

22. $8 + 8 = 16$ so $8 + 9 =$ _____

23. $6 + 6 = 12$ so $6 + 8 =$ _____

24. $5 + 5 = 10$ so $5 + 7 =$ _____

25. $4 + 4 = 8$ so $4 + 7 =$ _____

26. $7 + 7 = 14$ so $7 + 9 =$ _____

27. $6 + 6 = 12$ so $6 + 9 =$ _____

Doubles on the Brain

Directions:

Look at the number sentences. Circle true or false for each sentence. Then, use doubles to rewrite the false number sentences so that they are all true.

1. $7 + 7 = 10 + 4$ true   false   _____

2. $4 + 8 = 4 + 4 + 4$ true   false   _____

3. $5 + 9 = 5 + 5 + 5$ true   false   _____

4. $8 + 9 = 8 + 8 + 1$ true   false   _____

5. $4 + 9 = 4 + 4 + 5$ true   false   _____

6. $5 + 6 = 5 + 5 + 2$ true   false   _____

7. $6 + 8 = 6 + 6 + 1$ true   false   _____

8. $7 + 9 = 7 + 7 + 2$ true   false   _____

9. $8 + 8 = 7 + 7 + 2$ true   false   _____

10. $9 + 9 = 6 + 6 + 3$ true   false   _____

11. $6 + 7 = 6 + 6 + 1$ true   false   _____

12. $4 + 7 = 4 + 4 + 4$ true   false   _____

13. $5 + 8 = 5 + 5 + 3$ true   false   _____

14. $6 + 9 = 6 + 6 + 2$ true   false   _____

15. $9 + 9 = 8 + 8 + 2$ true   false   _____

16. $7 + 8 = 7 + 7 + 1$ true   false   _____

Ten Is Your Friend

Directions:
Adding 10 to a number is easy! Add 10 at the top of the page. Then, use 10 to help you add 9.

1. $1 + 10 =$ _____

2. $2 + 10 =$ _____

3. $4 + 10 =$ _____

4. $3 + 10 =$ _____

5. $5 + 10 =$ _____

6. $7 + 10 =$ _____

7. $6 + 10 =$ _____

8. $8 + 10 =$ _____

9. $9 + 10 =$ _____

10. $10 + 10 =$ _____

11. $12 + 10 =$ _____

12. $11 + 10 =$ _____

13. $13 + 10 =$ _____

14. $25 + 10 =$ _____

15. $34 + 10 =$ _____

16. $4 + 9$: Start with 4. Add 10. Subtract 1. $4 + 9 =$ _____

17. $2 + 9$: Start with 2. Add 10. Subtract 1. $2 + 9 =$ _____

18. $6 + 9$: Start with 6. Add 10. Subtract 1. $6 + 9 =$ _____

19. $3 + 9$: Start with 3. Add 10. Subtract 1. $3 + 9 =$ _____

20. $8 + 9$: Start with 8. Add 10. Subtract 1. $8 + 9 =$ _____

21. $5 + 9$: Start with 5. Add 10. Subtract 1. $5 + 9 =$ _____

22. $7 + 9$: Start with 7. Add 10. Subtract 1. $7 + 9 =$ _____

23. $9 + 9$: Start with 9. Add 10. Subtract 1. $9 + 9 =$ _____

24. $14 + 9$: Start with 14. Add 10. Subtract 1. $14 + 9 =$ _____

25. $25 + 9$: Start with 25. Add 10. Subtract 1. $25 + 9 =$ _____

Ten Again

Directions:
Use 10 to help you decide which addition sentences with 9 are true. Circle them.

1. $4 + 9 = 13$

2. $6 + 9 = 16 - 1$

3. $8 + 9 = 18 - 1$

4. $5 + 9 = 14$

5. $7 + 9 = 16$

6. $2 + 9 = 12$

7. $3 + 9 = 13$

8. $9 + 9 = 19 - 1$

9. $14 + 9 = 24 - 1$

10. $16 + 9 = 25$

11. $18 + 9 = 28$

12. $12 + 9 = 22 - 1$

13. $25 + 9 = 35$

14. $28 + 9 = 38 - 1$

15. $32 + 9 = 42 - 1$

16. $44 + 9 = 52$

17. $57 + 9 = 66$

18. $73 + 9 = 83$

19. $86 + 9 = 96 - 1$

20. $98 + 9 = 107$

21. $74 + 9 = 83$

22. $83 + 9 = 90$

23. $92 + 9 = 100$

24. $95 + 9 = 104$

Name _____   Date _____

Take the Shortcut

Directions:

Practice combining numbers that add up to 10. Then, use the adding shortcut shown below to solve the remaining problems.

1. 1 + _____ = 10   2. 2 + _____ = 10   3. 8 + _____ = 10

4. 3 + _____ = 10   5. 5 + _____ = 10   6. 6 + _____ = 10

7. 7 + _____ = 10   8. 4 + _____ = 10   9. 9 + _____ = 10

Example:	Split the second addend so that part can be added to the first addend to make 10.	Add the second part of the number to 10.	Answer
7 + 8	7 + _3_ + _5_	10 + _5_	_15_
10. 6 + 9	6 + ____ + ____	10 + ____	____
11. 4 + 7	4 + ____ + ____	10 + ____	____
12. 8 + 5	8 + ____ + ____	10 + ____	____
13. 9 + 7	9 + ____ + ____	10 + ____	____
14. 8 + 8	8 + ____ + ____	10 + ____	____
15. 5 + 7	5 + ____ + ____	10 + ____	____
16. 8 + 6	8 + ____ + ____	10 + ____	____
17. 9 + 9	9 + ____ + ____	10 + ____	____
18. 4 + 8	4 + ____ + ____	10 + ____	____
19. 3 + 9	3 + ____ + ____	10 + ____	____
20. 7 + 7	7 + ____ + ____	10 + ____	____
21. 9 + 8	9 + ____ + ____	10 + ____	____

Go Higher!

Directions:
The add-up-to-10 shortcut can be used with multiples of 10 to add higher numbers. Look at the example, then use the shortcut to solve the problems.

Example:	**Split the second addend so that part can be added to the first addend to make a multiple of 10.**	**Add the second part of the number to the multiple of 10.**	**Answer**
35 + 8	35 + __5__ + __3__	40 + __3__	__43__
1. 15 + 9	15 + ____ + ____	20 + ____	____
2. 24 + 7	24 + ____ + ____	30 + ____	____
3. 35 + 7	35 + ____ + ____	40 + ____	____
4. 46 + 8	46 + ____ + ____	50 + ____	____
5. 57 + 9	57 + ____ + ____	60 + ____	____
6. 69 + 4	69 + ____ + ____	70 + ____	____
7. 78 + 6	78 + ____ + ____	80 + ____	____

8. 16 + 5 = _____

9. 33 + 9 = _____

10. 28 + 4 = _____

11. 49 + 5 = _____

12. 46 + 6 = _____

13. 65 + 8 = _____

14. 57 + 4 = _____

15. 19 + 7 = _____

16. 24 + 9 = _____

17. 37 + 5 = _____

18. 52 + 9 = _____

19. 78 + 8 = _____

Using the Shortcut

Mathematical Relationships

Directions:
Circle the true number sentences.

1. $36 + 8 = 40 + 4$

2. $8 + 8 = 10 + 5$

3. $7 + 9 = 7 + 3 + 5$

4. $17 + 4 = 17 + 3 + 1$

5. $8 + 6 = 8 + 2 + 4$

6. $26 + 9 = 30 + 4$

7. $15 + 9 = 20 + 4$

8. $7 + 8 = 14$

9. $28 + 4 = 33$

10. $34 + 7 = 40 + 1$

11. $43 + 9 = 50 + 2$

12. $6 + 6 = 6 + 4 + 2$

13. $56 + 7 = 62$

14. $45 + 8 = 50 + 4$

15. $48 + 8 = 50 + 6$

16. $54 + 8 = 60 + 2$

17. $65 + 7 = 73$

18. $9 + 8 = 10 + 7$

19. $9 + 9 = 10 + 8$

20. $77 + 5 = 80 + 5$

21. $64 + 9 = 70 + 3$

22. $5 + 9 = 10 + 4$

23. $27 + 7 = 30 + 7$

24. $85 + 6 = 90 + 1$

Name That Sign

Mathematical Relationships

Directions:
Fill in each circle with a plus or minus sign to make a true number sentence.

1. $3 \bigcirc 4 = 7$

2. $8 = 9 \bigcirc 1$

3. $5 = 9 \bigcirc 4$

4. $7 \bigcirc 3 = 10$

5. $12 \bigcirc 3 = 9$

6. $13 = 6 \bigcirc 7$

7. $8 = 13 \bigcirc 5$

8. $17 \bigcirc 8 = 9$

9. $6 \bigcirc 8 = 14$

10. $15 = 6 \bigcirc 9$

11. $9 = 18 \bigcirc 9$

12. $13 \bigcirc 13 = 0$

13. $12 \bigcirc 12 = 24$

14. $7 = 15 \bigcirc 8$

15. $30 = 7 \bigcirc 23$

16. $50 \bigcirc 1 = 49$

17. $25 = 25 \bigcirc 0$

18. $35 = 70 \bigcirc 35$

19. $9 \bigcirc 51 = 60$

20. $2 = 100 \bigcirc 98$

Don't Add or Subtract!

Directions:
Write an equal or not equal sign in each circle. Just look at the numbers. Try not to actually add and subtract.

1. $5 + 3 \bigcirc 3 + 5$

2. $6 + 7 \bigcirc 7 + 7$

3. $3 + 3 \bigcirc 4 + 4$

4. $5 + 4 \bigcirc 6 + 3$

5. $7 - 3 \bigcirc 7 - 4$

6. $8 - 3 \bigcirc 7 - 2$

7. $8 - 8 \bigcirc 10 - 10$

8. $9 - 3 \bigcirc 8 - 3$

9. $3 + 4 \bigcirc 3 + 4$

10. $10 - 5 \bigcirc 10 - 2$

11. $10 - 4 \bigcirc 9 - 4$

12. $3 + 3 \bigcirc 4 + 3$

13. $10 - 5 \bigcirc 10 + 5$

14. $9 - 2 \bigcirc 9 - 2$

15. $6 + 8 \bigcirc 7 + 7$

16. $8 - 4 \bigcirc 8 - 5$

17. $11 - 4 \bigcirc 12 - 4$

18. $4 + 4 \bigcirc 4 + 2 + 2$

Name _____   Date _____

Mental Math Blastoff

Directions:

Use mental math to find the missing number in each number sentence below.

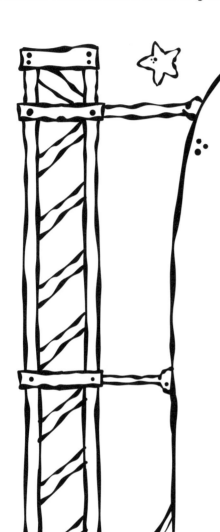

1. $12 + 13 = 13 +$ _____

2. $12 + 13 = 11 +$ _____

3. $25 + 36 = 24 +$ _____

4. $25 + 36 = 26 +$ _____

5. $37 + 55 = 35 +$ _____

6. $37 + 55 = 38 +$ _____

7. $64 + 36 = 63 +$ _____

8. $64 + 36 = 60 +$ _____

9. $14 - 6 = 13 -$ _____

10. $14 - 6 = 15 -$ _____

11. $23 - 7 = 22 -$ _____

12. $23 - 7 = 25 -$ _____

13. $36 - 19 = 34 -$ _____

14. $36 - 19 = 37 -$ _____

15. $72 - 28 = 71 -$ _____

16. $72 - 28 = 75 -$ _____

17. $83 + 17 = 82 +$ _____

18. $83 + 17 = 17 +$ _____

Don't Add!

Directions:
Circle true or false for each number sentence. Just look at the numbers. Try not to actually add.

1. 28 + 32 = 32 + 28   true   false

2. 19 + 17 = 18 + 18   true   false

3. 15 + 27 = 15 + 10 + 7   true   false

4. 30 + 24 = 30 + 20 + 4   true   false

5. 25 + 38 = 20 + 5 + 30 + 8   true   false

6. 27 + 46 = 28 + 47   true   false

7. 16 + 29 = 10 + 20 + 6 + 6   true   false

8. 24 + 36 = 26 + 34   true   false

9. 39 + 39 = 38 + 40   true   false

10. 56 + 29 = 50 + 20 + 6 + 9   true   false

11. 43 + 48 = 40 + 40 + 3 + 3   true   false

12. 248 + 365 = 265 + 348   true   false

13. 325 + 78 = 324 + 79   true   false

14. 226 + 157 = 225 + 156   true   false

15. 456 + 139 = 500 + 80 + 6 + 9   true   false

16. 366 + 148 = 365 + 150   true   false

Name _____   Date _____

Hundreds Are Your Friends

Directions:

Which is easier to figure out in your head: 99 + 99 or 100 + 100 – 2? Adding 99 is easy if you change the 99 to 100 and subtract 1. Try this shortcut below. Then, try it with 95. Just subtract 5 instead of 1.

		Change each 99 to 100. **Subtract 1 for each 99 changed.**	**Answer**
1.	99 + 99 + 99	100 + 100 + 100 – 3	_____
2.	99 + 199	100 + 200 – 2	_____
3.	199 + 199	200 + 200 – 2	_____
4.	99 + 299	100 + 300 – 2	_____
5.	99 + 199 + 299	100 + 200 + 300 – 3	_____

		Change each 95 to 100. **Subtract 5 for each 95 changed.**	**Answer**
6.	95 + 95	100 + 100 – 10	_____
7.	95 + 195	100 + 200 – 10	_____
8.	195 + 195	200 + 200 – 10	_____
9.	95 + 195 + 195	100 + 200 + 200 – 15	_____
10.	95 + 195 + 295	100 + 200 + 300 – 15	_____

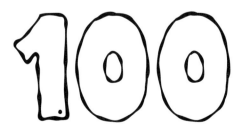

Name _____ Date _____

Doughnut Decimals

Directions:
Use the hundreds shortcut to figure out how much each person spent on doughnuts.

Example:
Joe bought 2 boxes of Crunchy Doughnuts. How much did he spend? $3.98
Think: 199 + 199 = 200 + 200 – 2

Plain	Crunchy	Cream	Everything
$0.99	$1.99	$2.95	$3.95

1. Sue bought 3 boxes of Plain Doughnuts. How much did she spend? _____

2. Rod bought 2 boxes of Cream Doughnuts. How much did he spend? _____

3. Kira bought 3 boxes of Everything Doughnuts. How much did she spend? _____

4. Sean bought 4 boxes of Crunchy Doughnuts. How much did he spend? _____

5. Jamal bought 5 boxes of Plain Doughnuts. How much did he spend? _____

6. Suki bought 1 box of Crunchy and 1 box of Plain. How much did she spend? _____

7. Parker bought 1 box of Cream and 1 box of Everything. How much did he spend? _____

8. Emma bought 1 box of Crunchy and 1 box of Cream. How much did she spend? _____

9. Michael bought 1 box of Plain and 1 box of Everything. How much did he spend? _____

Tricky Times

Directions:

Many of these number sentences are true, but some are false. Use what you know about multiplication to find the false ones and cross them out.

1. $5 \times 6 = 6 \times 5$

2. $3 \times 8 = 8 + 8 + 8$

3. $4 \times 7 = 7 + 7 + 7 + 4$

4. $4 \times 9 = 18 + 18$

5. $6 \times 6 = 6 + 6$

6. $7 \times 7 = 35 + 7 + 7$

7. $5 \times 8 = 25 + 40$

8. $6 \times 8 = 24 + 24$

9. $9 \times 5 = 18 + 18 + 15$

10. $8 \times 7 = 40 + 8 + 8$

11. $9 \times 9 = 45 + 36$

12. $8 \times 8 = 32 + 32$

13. $9 \times 6 = 96$

14. $7 \times 9 = 35 + 18$

15. $5 \times 12 = 30 + 30$

16. $8 \times 13 = 80 + 24$

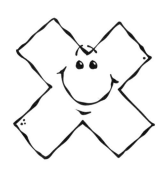

Equal or Not Equal?

Mathematical Relationships

Directions:
Write an equal or not equal sign in each circle.

1. $3 + 7$ ◯ $15 - 5$

2. 6×2 ◯ $7 + 7$

3. $9 + 6$ ◯ $8 + 7$

4. $8 + 4$ ◯ $4 + 8$

5. $7 + 7$ ◯ $7 + 8$

6. 7×4 ◯ 14×2

7. 3×4 ◯ 6×2

8. 8×6 ◯ 6×8

9. 5×5 ◯ 6×5

10. $20 - 6$ ◯ $20 - 7$

11. $10 - 4$ ◯ $10 - 5$

12. 8×4 ◯ $16 + 16$

13. $10 - 5$ ◯ $10 + 5$

14. 6×1 ◯ $12 - 7$

15. 3×2 ◯ $15 \div 5$

16. $18 \div 6$ ◯ $18 \div 3$

17. $18 - 9$ ◯ $10 - 1$

18. 3×2 ◯ $12 \div 2$

19. $20 \div 4$ ◯ $3 + 2$

20. $12 \div 3$ ◯ $12 \div 4$

Assigning Signs

Directions:
Decide which signs (+, −, x, or ÷) go in the circles. Each box should have 1 of each sign.

1. 6 ◯ 1 = 6

2. 6 ◯ 1 = 7

3. 6 ◯ 1 = 6

4. 6 ◯ 1 = 5

5. 4 ◯ 4 = 0

6. 4 ◯ 4 = 1

7. 4 ◯ 4 = 16

8. 4 ◯ 4 = 8

9. 9 ◯ 3 = 3

10. 9 ◯ 3 = 6

11. 9 ◯ 3 = 27

12. 9 ◯ 3 = 12

13. 8 ◯ 2 = 16

14. 8 ◯ 2 = 6

15. 8 ◯ 2 = 4

16. 8 ◯ 2 = 10

17. 12 ◯ 4 = 16

18. 12 ◯ 4 = 48

19. 12 ◯ 4 = 3

20. 12 ◯ 4 = 8

21. 10 ◯ 1 = 10

22. 10 ◯ 1 = 11

23. 10 ◯ 1 = 10

24. 10 ◯ 1 = 9

Name _____ Date _____

Strawberry Shortcut

Directions:
Use any of the shortcuts you have learned to figure out the answers in your head. For each problem, shade in a strawberry below with the correct answer.

1. $6 + 9 =$ _____

2. $5 + 6 =$ _____

3. $8 + 5 =$ _____

4. $8 + 8 =$ _____

5. $7 + 9 =$ _____

6. $9 + 9 =$ _____

7. $5 + 9 =$ _____

8. $7 + 7 =$ _____

9. $6 + 6 =$ _____

10. $8 + 9 =$ _____

11. $6 + 7 =$ _____

12. $8 + 7 =$ _____

13. $14 + 8 =$ _____

14. $16 + 9 =$ _____

15. $13 + 8 =$ _____

16. $15 + 7 =$ _____

17. $17 + 4 =$ _____

18. $18 + 6 =$ _____

19. $27 + 8 =$ _____

20. $24 + 9 =$ _____

21. $28 + 3 =$ _____

22. $35 + 6 =$ _____

23. $37 + 9 =$ _____

24. $39 + 5 =$ _____

25. $47 + 6 =$ _____

26. $44 + 8 =$ _____

27. $48 + 7 =$ _____

Solve These Sentences

Directions:

Figure out the missing number for each sentence.

1. $3 \times \underline{\hspace{1cm}} = 12$

2. $16 = 4 \times \underline{\hspace{1cm}}$

3. $\underline{\hspace{1cm}} \times 2 = 8$

4. $10 = \underline{\hspace{1cm}} \times 5$

5. $6 \times 4 = \underline{\hspace{1cm}}$

6. $\underline{\hspace{1cm}} = 5 \times 9$

7. $6 \times \underline{\hspace{1cm}} = 18$

8. $35 = 7 \times \underline{\hspace{1cm}}$

9. $\underline{\hspace{1cm}} \times 4 = 32$

10. $30 = \underline{\hspace{1cm}} \times 15$

11. $16 \div \underline{\hspace{1cm}} = 2$

12. $1 = 8 \div \underline{\hspace{1cm}}$

13. $20 \div 5 = \underline{\hspace{1cm}}$

14. $\underline{\hspace{1cm}} = 42 \div 6$

15. $\underline{\hspace{1cm}} \div 4 = 3$

16. $2 = \underline{\hspace{1cm}} \div 7$

17. $28 \div \underline{\hspace{1cm}} = 7$

18. $4 = 36 \div \underline{\hspace{1cm}}$

19. $\underline{\hspace{1cm}} \div 2 = 3$

20. $5 = \underline{\hspace{1cm}} \div 3$

21. $\underline{\hspace{1cm}} \times 3 = 21$

22. $72 = 9 \times \underline{\hspace{1cm}}$

23. $\underline{\hspace{1cm}} \div 4 = 10$

24. $8 = \underline{\hspace{1cm}} \div 2$

Double Trouble

Solving Number Sentences

Directions:

Fill in the missing number in each number sentence.

1. $3 \times 7 = \rule{1cm}{0.4pt} \times 3$

2. $5 \times 3 = \rule{1cm}{0.4pt} \times 15$

3. $\rule{1cm}{0.4pt} \times 4 = 4 \times 6$

4. $1 \times \rule{1cm}{0.4pt} = 4 \times 4$

5. $6 \times 2 = \rule{1cm}{0.4pt} \times 4$

6. $8 \times 3 = \rule{1cm}{0.4pt} \times 6$

7. $7 \times \rule{1cm}{0.4pt} = 3 \times 14$

8. $9 \times 7 = \rule{1cm}{0.4pt} \times 9$

9. $6 \times 5 = \rule{1cm}{0.4pt} \times 1$

10. $\rule{1cm}{0.4pt} \times 5 = 4 \times 10$

11. $12 \times \rule{1cm}{0.4pt} = 3 \times 4$

12. $\rule{1cm}{0.4pt} \times 6 = 6 \times 8$

13. $12 \div 4 = 15 \div \rule{1cm}{0.4pt}$

14. $24 \div 6 = \rule{1cm}{0.4pt} \div 1$

15. $16 \div 2 = 8 \div \rule{1cm}{0.4pt}$

16. $7 \div 1 = \rule{1cm}{0.4pt} \div 2$

17. $10 \div \rule{1cm}{0.4pt} = 4 \div 2$

18. $\rule{1cm}{0.4pt} \div 5 = 12 \div 6$

19. $20 \div \rule{1cm}{0.4pt} = 10 \div 2$

20. $\rule{1cm}{0.4pt} \div 3 = 15 \div 5$

21. $12 \div 2 = \rule{1cm}{0.4pt} \div 3$

22. $\rule{1cm}{0.4pt} \div 4 = 8 \div 2$

23. $14 \div 7 = \rule{1cm}{0.4pt} \div 4$

24. $\rule{1cm}{0.4pt} \div 9 = 2 \div 1$

Name _____   Date _____

Be a Math Detective

Directions:

Investigate these math problems. Don't be fooled by different signs.
Write the answers on the lines.

1. 2 + 2 = _____	5. 3 + 3 = _____
2. 2 - 2 = _____	6. 3 - 3 = _____
3. 2 x 2 = _____	7. 3 x 3 = _____
4. 2 ÷ 2 = _____	8. 3 ÷ 3 = _____
9. 4 + 4 = _____	13. 5 + 5 = _____
10. 4 - 4 = _____	14. 5 - 5 = _____
11. 4 x 4 = _____	15. 5 x 5 = _____
12. 4 ÷ 4 = _____	16. 5 ÷ 5 = _____
17. 6 + 6 = _____	21. 7 + 7 = _____
18. 6 - 6 = _____	22. 7 - 7 = _____
19. 6 x 6 = _____	23. 7 x 7 = _____
20. 6 ÷ 6 = _____	24. 7 ÷ 7 = _____
25. 8 + 8 = _____	29. 9 + 9 = _____
26. 8 - 8 = _____	30. 9 - 9 = _____
27. 8 x 8 = _____	31. 9 x 9 = _____
28. 8 ÷ 8 = _____	32. 9 ÷ 9 = _____

Name _____   Date _____

Mathman vs. Arithmewoman

Directions:
Circle the correct answer in each box.

1. _____ + 4 = 12 Mathman says 16. Arithmewoman says 8.	**2.** 15 = _____ + 9 Mathman says 6. Arithmewoman says 24.
3. 15 – _____ = 11 Mathman says 4. Arithmewoman says 26.	**4.** 8 = 14 – _____ Mathman says 22. Arithmewoman says 6.
5. _____ – 5 = 9 Mathman says 4. Arithmewoman says 14.	**6.** 8 = _____ – 4 Mathman says 12. Arithmewoman says 4.
7. 6 x _____ = 12 Mathman says 2. Arithmewoman says 72.	**8.** 20 = 10 x _____ Mathman says 200. Arithmewoman says 2.
9. 30 ÷ _____ = 10 Mathman says 3. Arithmewoman says 300.	**10.** 6 = 24 ÷ _____ Mathman says 144. Arithmewoman says 4.
11. _____ ÷ 6 = 3 Mathman says 2. Arithmewoman says 18.	**12.** 8 = _____ ÷ 4 Mathman says 32. Arithmewoman says 2.
13. 17 + _____ = 30 Mathman says 47. Arithmewoman says 13.	**14.** 6 = _____ – 14 Mathman says 20. Arithmewoman says 8.
15. _____ x 5 = 10 Mathman says 2. Arithmewoman says 50.	**16.** 8 = _____ ÷ 2 Mathman says 4. Arithmewoman says 16.

Name _____ Date _____

Turtle Twins

Directions:
Two turtles in each row are twins because their answers are equal. Circle the twins and write them in a number sentence.

1.   　　　　　_____ = _____

2.  　　　　　_____ = _____

3.   　　　　　_____ = _____

4.   　　　　　_____ = _____

5.

6.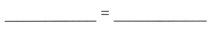

7.    　　_____ = _____

8.    　　_____ = _____

9.  　　_____ = _____

Turtle Triplets

 Equality

Directions:

Three turtles in each row are triplets because their answers are equal. Circle the triplets.

1.  5 x 1    10 – 2    2 + 3   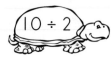 10 ÷ 2    12 – 6

2.  6 + 6    12 – 2   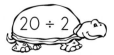 20 ÷ 2    5 + 2    5 x 2

3.  16 ÷ 2   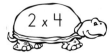 2 x 4    12 – 6    3 x 3    5 + 3

4. 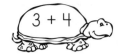 3 + 4    12 ÷ 2    10 – 3    2 x 3    6 ÷ 1

5.  4 ÷ 4    4 + 1    20 ÷ 5    10 – 6    2 x 2

6.  4 + 4   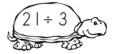 21 ÷ 3    6 + 1    1 x 7   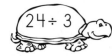 24 ÷ 3

7. 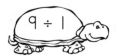 9 ÷ 1   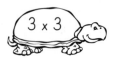 3 x 3   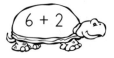 6 + 2   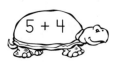 5 + 4    2 x 4

8.  10 – 9    1 + 1    6 ÷ 6    20 – 18    1 x 1

9.  12 ÷ 6    3 + 5   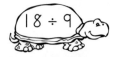 18 ÷ 9    10 – 8   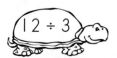 12 ÷ 3

Treasure Tiles

Equality

Directions:

Pirates buried treasure under a tile in this treasure room. They booby-trapped some tiles so that they would break and fall. Find the safe path by shading all of the tiles that equal 12.

Start 6 + 6	3 x 4	13 – 1	15 – 2	6 x 4	8 + 5	12 – 1	13 – 2
30 – 12	6 + 7	20 – 8	6 x 3	17 – 4	20 ÷ 2	6 x 6	9 + 9
25 – 14	5 x 3	6 x 2	8 + 4	12 ÷ 1	7 + 5	9 + 4	10 x 2
6 + 8	22 ÷ 2	20 – 7	12 ÷ 2	4 x 4	12 – 0	12 x 2	8 – 4
36 ÷ 4	12 – 6	12 x 12	8 ÷ 4	30 – 8	18 – 6	12 x 1	7 x 2
10 + 3	12 ÷ 3	12 x 0	14 – 1	6 ÷ 6	2 x 4	11 + 1	20 – 7
18 ÷ 3	9 x 3	6 + 5	3 x 3	10 ÷ 2	1 x 2	24 ÷ 2	3 + 9
1 + 12	8 + 2	2 x 9	15 – 4	24 ÷ 3	7 + 4	8 x 2	Finish 36 ÷ 3

Equal Schmequal

This is a game for 2 players.

Directions:

1. Cut out the playing cards below and the scorecards on page 107.
2. Turn the playing cards upside down and mix them up.
3. Take turns drawing one card at a time.
4. If you have two cards with equal amounts, put them in two of the boxes on your scorecard. If you have two cards with unequal amounts, place the cards facedown in their original positions.
5. The first player to fill up all of the boxes on her scorecard wins.

5 ÷ 1	48 ÷ 6	10 ÷ 2	4 x 2
24 ÷ 4	7 ÷ 1	1 x 7	36 ÷ 9
15 ÷ 3	16 ÷ 2	1 x 8	49 ÷ 7
16 ÷ 4	56 ÷ 8	5 x 1	6 x 3
3 x 3	27 ÷ 3	2 x 9	2 x 3
24 ÷ 8	6 ÷ 2	4 x 5	10 x 2

Equal Schmequal Scorecards

Equality

_____'s **Equal Schmequal Scorecard**

[ ] = [ ]

[ ] = [ ]

[ ] = [ ]

_____'s **Equal Schmequal Scorecard**

[ ] = [ ]

[ ] = [ ]

[ ] = [ ]

Name _____   Date _____

Growing Triangles

Directions:
Follow the directions below.

A

Shade this triangle on the top of the next one. (This one has been done for you as an example.)

B

Shade this triangle on the top of the next one. (This one has been done for you as an example.)

C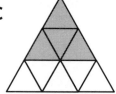

Shade this triangle on the top of the next one. (This one has been done for you as an example.)

D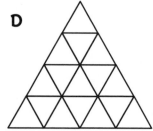

Shade this triangle on the top of the next one.

E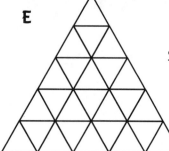

Shade this triangle on the top of the next one.

F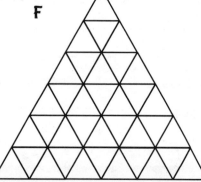

Complete this chart.

	A	**B**	**C**	**D**	**E**	**F**
Triangles on each side	1	2	3			
Total small triangles	1	4				
Triangles in bottom row	1	3				

Use the pictures of the triangles to complete the pattern.

(1) (4) (9) ( ) ( ) ( ) ( )

© Carson-Dellosa   108   Elementary Algebra • CD-104105

Growing Squares

Directions:

Follow the directions below.

A Shade this square on the upper left corner of the next one. (This one has been done for you as an example.)

B Shade this square on the upper left corner of the next one. (This one has been done for you as an example.)

C Shade this square on the upper left corner of the next one.

D Shade this square on the upper left corner of the next one.

E Shade this square on the upper left corner of the next one.

F

Complete this chart.

	A	B	C	D	E	F
Squares on each side	1	2	3			
Total small squares	1	4				
Squares not shaded	1					

Use the pictures of the squares to complete the pattern.

○ 1   +__−__   ○ 4   +__−__   ○ 9   +__−__   ○   +__−__   ○   +__−__   ○   +__−__   ○

Name _____   Date _____

★ Investigating Change

Directions:

Party Mart rents square folding tables. Look at the seating arrangements and complete the chart to tell how many people can sit at each group of tables. Then, answer the questions below.

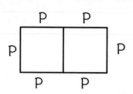

1 table seats 4 people   2 tables seat 6 people

Number of Tables	People Seated
1	4
2	6
3	
4	

1. How many tables does it take to seat 12 people? _____

2. How many tables does it take to seat 20 people? _____

3. How many people are able to sit at 4 tables? _____

4. How many people are able to sit at 8 tables? _____

Table Trick: If you multiply the number of tables by 2 and then add 2, you get the number of people who can sit at them. Try this trick with the next problems.

5. How many people are able to sit at 6 tables? _____

6. How many people are able to sit at 20 tables? _____

7. How many people are able to sit at 100 tables? _____

Rectangular Party Tables

Directions:

Party Mart also rents rectangular folding tables. Look at the seating arrangements and complete the chart to tell how many people can sit at each group of tables. Then, answer the questions below.

1 table seats 6 people

2 tables seat 10 people

Number of Tables	People Seated
1	6
2	10
3	
4	

1. How many tables does it take to seat 18 people? _____

2. How many tables does it take to seat 38 people? _____

3. How many people are able to sit at 5 tables? _____

4. How many people are able to sit at 10 tables? _____

Table Trick: If you multiply the number of tables by 4 and then add 2, you get the number of people who can sit at them. Try this trick with the next problems.

5. How many people are able to sit at 6 tables? _____

6. How many people are able to sit at 20 tables? _____

7. How many people are able to sit at 100 tables? _____

Name _____   Date _____

Monster Icicle!

Directions:

Tyler found a huge icicle outside his window. He and his dad measured it each day for 10 days using a ladder and a tape measure. They made a chart of their measurements. Use the chart to complete the graph. The first 2 days have been done for you. Then, answer the questions below.

Our Monster Icicle

Day	1	2	3	4	5	6	7	8	9	10
Length (inches)	5	7	6	10	15	11	16	20	26	34

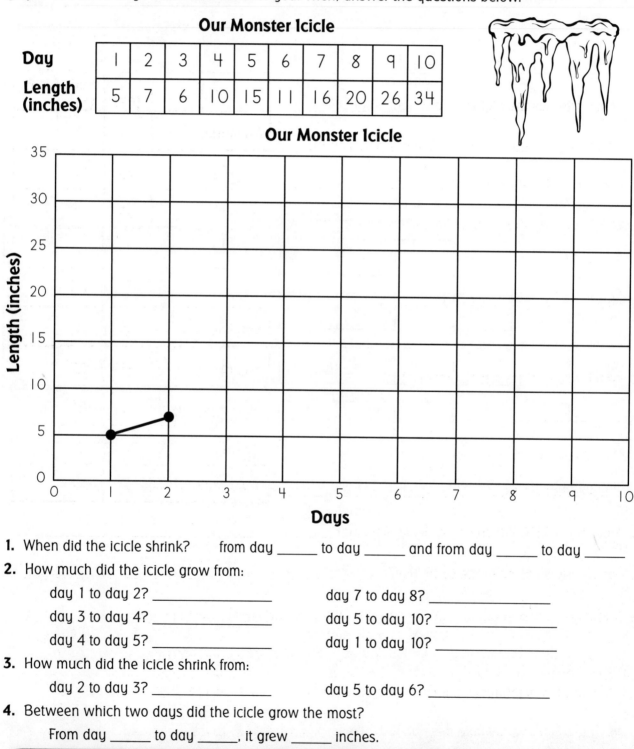

Our Monster Icicle

1. When did the icicle shrink?   from day _____ to day _____ and from day _____ to day _____

2. How much did the icicle grow from:

   day 1 to day 2? _____   day 7 to day 8? _____

   day 3 to day 4? _____   day 5 to day 10? _____

   day 4 to day 5? _____   day 1 to day 10? _____

3. How much did the icicle shrink from:

   day 2 to day 3? _____   day 5 to day 6? _____

4. Between which two days did the icicle grow the most?

   From day _____ to day _____, it grew _____ inches.

Name _____   Date _____

High and Low across the U.S.A.

Directions:

Below is a chart with the high and low temperatures in degrees Fahrenheit in 10 U.S. cities on a day in November. Complete the difference column on the chart, then answer the questions.

1. Which city has the lowest low? _____

2. Which city has the highest high? _____

3. Which city has the smallest difference between the low and high temperatures? _____

4. Which city has the largest difference between the low and high temperatures? _____

5. Which city or cities has the highest low?

   _____

6. Which city or cities has the lowest high?

   _____

7. What is the difference between the lowest low and the highest high? _____

City	Low (°F)	High (°F)	Diff.
Anchorage	16	25	
Chicago	45	59	
Denver	33	57	
Honolulu	75	86	
Houston	62	80	
Los Angeles	55	68	
Miami	75	85	
New York City	42	53	
Seattle	44	51	
Washington, D.C.	41	59	

8. Freezing is 32°F. Which city is below freezing? _____

9. Which two cities have the same high? _____

10. Write the temperatures of the cities in order from lowest low to highest low.

    ____ ____ ____ ____ ____ ____ ____ ____ ____ ____

11. Write the temperatures of the cities in order from lowest high to highest high.

    ____ ____ ____ ____ ____ ____ ____ ____ ____ ____

Pet Problems

Directions:
Write a math sentence about each problem using the letters in the problem and a blank line (___) for what is not known.

Example:

Jamal had C cats and D dogs. How many cats and dogs did Jamal have altogether?

$$C + D = \underline{\quad\quad}$$

1. Sheria had F fish, but she gave S of them to her cousin. How many fish does Sheria have now?

   _____

2. Dominick had G guinea pigs and M mice. How many animals did Dominick have in all?

   _____

3. Reba had H hamsters. They had B babies. How many hamsters does she have now?

   _____

4. LaTasha had R rabbits. She gave away S of them. How many rabbits does she have now?

   _____

5. Luis had C cats. His aunt wanted S of them, so he gave them to her. How many cats does Luis have now?

   _____

6. Andrew had B birds, F ferrets, and H hamsters. How many animals did he have altogether?

   _____

7. Kaileigh had M mice, but S of them got out of their cage. How many mice are still in the cage?

   _____

Crazy Collections

Using Variables

Directions:

Write a math sentence about each problem using the letters in the problem and a blank line (____) for what is not known.

Example:

Triff the Troll collects snails. He has A aquariums with S snails in each. How many snails does Triff have in all?

$$A \times S = \underline{\hspace{1.5cm}}$$
_____

1. Trina Troll collects owls. She has H houses for them and W owls in each house. How many owls does she have?

_____

2. Tred collects bent nails. He has N nails. If he puts E number of nails in each can, how many cans will he need?

_____

3. Trilla collects feathers. She has B boxes with F feathers in each. How many feathers does she have altogether?

_____

4. Trini the Troll collects false mustaches. He has M mustaches. There are S mustaches in each box. How many boxes are there?

_____

5. Treeba collects rubber bands. He has R rubber bands. If he puts the same number in each of his C cans, how many should go in each can?

_____

6. Trill Troll collects worms. She has W worms. She has F worm farms. If she has the same number of worms on each farm, how many worms are in each farm?

_____

7. Troberta Troll collects marbles. She has M marbles in each box and she has B boxes. How many marbles does she have in all?

_____

Name _____ Date _____

Computer Games

Using Variables

Directions:

Tiara has some computer games. T stands for the number of computer games Tiara has. Kevin has 3 fewer games than Tiara does. K stands for the number of computer games Kevin has.

T – 3 = K   shows that the number of Tiara's games minus 3 equals the number of Kevin's games.

Complete the table to show how many computer games Kevin would have (K), if Tiara had T games. Then, answer the questions below.

If T is	3	4	5	6	7	8	9	10	11	12	13	14	15	16	17
then K is	0	1	2												

1. If Tiara has 5 games, how many does Kevin have? _____

2. If Tiara has 8 games, how many does Kevin have? _____

3. If Tiara has 18 games, how many does Kevin have? _____

4. If Kevin has 3 games, how many does Tiara have? _____

5. If Kevin has 10 games, how many does Tiara have? _____

6. If Kevin has 16 games, how many does Tiara have? _____

7. If Tiara has 100 games, how many does Kevin have? _____

8. If Tiara has 500 games, how many does Kevin have? _____

9. If Kevin has 100 games, how many does Tiara have? _____

10. If Kevin has 500 games, how many does Tiara have? _____

Name _____ Date _____

Letter and Number Sentences

Directions:
Complete each table and answer the questions.

A – B = 10

1. If A is 14, how much is B? _____

2. If B is 7, how much is A? _____

3. If A is 25, how much is B? _____

4. If B is 50, how much is A? _____

5. Why did A start at 10 in the table instead of 0 or 1?

   _____

   _____

   _____

If A is	then B is
10	0
11	
12	
13	
14	
15	
16	
17	
18	

C + D = 10

6. If C is 3, how much is D? _____

7. If D is 2, how much is C? _____

8. If C is 9, how much is D? _____

9. If D is 4, how much is C? _____

10. Can you continue this table? Why or why not?

    _____

    _____

    _____

If C is	then D is
0	
1	
2	
3	
4	
5	
6	
7	
8	
9	
10	

Letter and Number Puzzles

Directions:
The same letter stands for the same number. Figure out what number each letter stands for.

$8 = A + A$ $A = \rule{1cm}{0.4pt}$

$8 = A + B + B$ $B = \rule{1cm}{0.4pt}$

$8 = A + C + C + C + C$ $C = \rule{1cm}{0.4pt}$

1. How did you figure out A? _____

_____

2. How did you figure out B? _____

_____

3. How did you figure out C? _____

_____

· ·

$15 = D + D + D$ $D = \rule{1cm}{0.4pt}$

$15 = D + E$ $E = \rule{1cm}{0.4pt}$

$15 = E + F + F + F + F + F$ $F = \rule{1cm}{0.4pt}$

4. How did you figure out D? _____

_____

5. How did you figure out E? _____

_____

6. How did you figure out F? _____

_____

More Letter and Number Puzzles

Using Variables

Directions:
The same letter stands for the same number. Figure out what number each letter stands for.

$20 = J + J + J + J$ $J = $ _____

$14 = J + K + K + K$ $K = $ _____

$11 = K + L + L$ $L = $ _____

1. How did you figure out J? _____
    _____

2. How did you figure out K? _____
    _____

3. How did you figure out L? _____
    _____

4. Which of these sentences would also be true about J, K, and L? Circle them.

$J + J + K = 13$ $J + K + L = 11$

$J + L + L = 10$ $K + K + L = 10$

$J - L = 1$ $J - K = 8$

$L - K = 7$ $J - 2 = K$

$8 - J = K$ $L + 1 = J$

Note: When students are asked to write number sentences, any equation equivalent to the one listed is also correct.

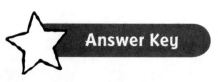

Page 5

1. ▲▲△▲▲△▲▲△▲▲△▲▲△▲
2. ▲△△▲△△▲△△▲△△▲△△▲
3. △▲▲△▲▲△▲▲△▲▲△▲▲
4. ▲△▲△▲△▲△▲△▲△▲△▲
5. ▲▲△▲▲△▲▲△▲▲△▲▲△
6. ▲△△▲△△▲△△▲△△▲△△
7. △▲▲△▲▲△▲▲△▲▲△▲▲△
8. ▲▲▲▲▲▲▲▲▲▲▲▲▲▲▲

Page 6

1. S, T, T, S, T, T, S, T, T, S, T, T, S, T, T, S, T, T, S, T, T, S, T
2. C, D, D, D, C, D, D, D, C, D, D, D, C, D, D, D, C, D, D, D, C, D, D, D
3. X, X, Y, Y, X, X, Y, Y, X, X, Y, Y, X, X, Y, Y, X, X, Y, Y, X, X, Y, Y
4. J, J, J, K, K, J, J, J, K, K, J, J, J, K, K, J, J, J, K, K, J, J
5. O, P, P, P, P, P, O, P, P, P, P, P, O, P, P, P, P, P, O, P
6. G, G, G, H, G, G, G, H, G, G, G, H, G, G, G, H, G, G, G, H, G, G, G, H
7. M, N, N, O, O, O, M, N, N, O, O, O, M, N, N, O, O, O, M, N
8. U, U, V, W, W, U, U, V, W, W, U, U, V, W, W, U, U, V, W, W, U, U
9. A, B, B, B, B, C, A, B, B, B, B, C, A, B, B, B, B, C, A, B
10. P, P, P, Q, R, P

Page 7

1. 6, 6, 7, 7, 8, 8, 9, 9, 10, 10
2. 7, 7, 8, 9, 9, 10, 11, 11, 12, 13
3. 7, 8, 8, 8, 9, 10, 10, 10, 11
4. 7, 7, 7, 8, 9, 9, 9, 10, 11
5. 5, 5, 5, 6, 6, 7, 7, 7, 8, 8
6. 5, 5, 6, 6, 6, 6, 7, 7, 8
7. 10, 11, 11, 12, 12, 13, 14, 14
8. 7, 7, 7, 8, 8, 9, 10, 10, 10
9. 10, 11, 11, 12, 13, 14, 14, 15, 16
10. 7, 8, 8, 9, 9, 9, 10, 11, 11

Page 8

1. △ 2. ◹
3. ◁ 4. ▷
5. △• 6. △
7. ▲ 8. ▲

Page 9

1. 13, 15, 17, 19, 21, 23
2. 14, 16, 18, 20, 22, 24
3. 30, 35, 40, 45, 50, 55
4. 50, 60, 70, 80, 90, 100
5. 51, 61, 71, 81, 91
6. 56, 67, 78, 89, 100
7. 57, 67, 77, 87, 97
8. 55, 64, 73, 82, 91

Page 10

1. upper left box should be shaded; shaded square moves in a clockwise direction around the grid
2. M, N, N, O, O, O; alphabet in the pattern of 1 letter, 2 letters, 3 letters, 1 letter, 2 letters, etc.
3. 2 upright triangles and 2 upside-down triangles
4. 99, 108; count by 9s
5. 17, 18; add 1 then add 2

Page 11

1. circle, circle, square; 2 circles, 1 square repeats
2. AABAABAAB
3. 2 of the same item and 1 different item repeats
4. circle, triangle, square; pattern as described repeats
5. ABCABCABC
6. 3 different items repeat

Page 12

Answers will vary.

Page 13

Patterns should be completed.
1. 4   2. 14
3. 24   4. 8
5. 11   6. 15
7. 12   8. 27
9. 36   10. 8
11. 11   12. 13

Page 14
Patterns should be completed.

1. 16	2. 32
3. 52	4. 5
5. 9	6. 12
7. 30	8. 50
9. 60	10. 9
11. 11	12. 14

Page 15
Patterns should be completed.

1. 30	2. 66
3. 72	4. 7
5. 9	6. 13
7. 35	8. 56
9. 84	10. 7
11. 9	12. 14

Page 16
Patterns should be completed.

1. 48	2. 80
3. 96	4. 5
5. 11	6. 13
7. 45	8. 63
9. 108	10. 8
11. 9	12. 13

Page 17
Patterns should be completed.

1. 80	2. 110
3. 130	4. 9
5. 10	6. 12
7. 77	8. 110
9. 132	10. 9
11. 11	12. 13

Page 18
Multiplication table should be completed.
1., 3., 5., 7., 9. both
2., 4., 6., 8., 10. even

Page 19
dimes to nickels: 4, 6, 8, 10, 12, 14, 16, 18, 20
quarters to nickels: 10, 15, 20, 25, 30, 35, 40, 45, 50
dollars to quarters: 8, 12, 16, 20, 24, 28, 32, 36, 40
dollars to dimes: 20, 30, 40, 50, 60, 70, 80, 90, 100
dollars to nickels: 40, 60, 80, 100, 120, 140, 160, 180, 200

1. 16 nickels	2. 30 nickels
3. 16 quarters	4. 70 dimes
5. 100 nickels	

Page 20

1. 40¢ or $0.40	2. 60¢ or $0.60
3. 100¢ or $1.00	4. 150¢ or $1.50
5. 500¢ or $5.00	6. 60¢ or $0.60
7. 100¢ or $1.00	8. 150¢ or $1.50
9. 200¢ or $2.00	10. 1,000¢ or $10.00
11. 75¢ or $0.75	12. 150¢ or $1.50
13. 200¢ or $2.00	14. 500¢ or $5.00
15. 2,500¢ or $25.00	

Page 21

1. 30, 50, 80	2. 50, 40, 90
3. 20, 50, 70	4. 10, 20, 50, 80
5. 15, 30, 50, 95	6. Bozo
7. Doofus & Goofus	8. 60¢
9. 10¢	10. Twerpy

Page 22
1. 1, 2, 3, 4, 5, 6, 7, 8, 9, 10, 11
2. 3, 5, 7, 9, 11, 13, 15, 17, 19, 21, 23
3. 3, 6, 9, 12, 15, 18, 21, 24, 27, 30, 33
4. 4, 7, 10, 13, 16, 19, 22, 25, 28, 31, 34
5. 5, 8, 11, 14, 17, 20, 23, 26, 29, 32, 35
6. 4, 8, 12, 16, 20, 24, 28, 32, 36, 40, 44

Page 23
1. 5, 9, 13, 17, 21, 25, 29, 33, 37, 41, 45
2. 6, 10, 14, 18, 22, 26, 30, 34, 38, 42, 46
3. 7, 11, 15, 19, 23, 27, 31, 35, 39, 43, 47
4. 6, 11, 16, 21, 26, 31, 36, 41, 46, 51, 56
5. 8, 14, 20, 26, 32, 38, 44, 50, 56, 62, 68
6. 10, 17, 24, 31, 38, 45, 52, 59, 66, 73, 80
7. 12, 20, 28, 36, 44, 52, 60, 68, 76, 84, 92
8. 14, 23, 32, 41, 50, 59, 68, 77, 86, 95, 104

Page 24
1. +10; 42, 52, 62, 72, 82, 92, 102, 112
2. +10; 46, 56, 66, 76, 86, 96, 106, 116
3. +15; 75, 90, 105, 120, 135, 150, 165, 180
4. +20; 100, 120, 140, 160, 180, 200, 220, 240
5. +20; 83, 103, 123, 143, 163, 183, 203, 223
6. +25; 125, 150, 175, 200, 225, 250, 275, 300
7. +50; 250, 300, 350, 400, 450, 500, 550, 600
8. +30; 150, 180, 210, 240, 270, 300, 330, 360

Page 25

1. 11, 12, 16, 17, 21, 22, 26, 27
2. 12, 14, 17, 19, 22, 24, 27, 29
3. 16, 18, 23, 25, 30, 32, 37, 39
4. 23, 24, 34, 35, 45, 46, 56, 57
5. 19, 22, 28, 31, 37, 40, 46, 49
6. 35, 40, 50, 55, 65, 70, 80, 85

Page 26

1. +5
2. +2
3. +3
4. +10
5. +8
6. +3, +2
7. +1, +5
8. +4, +2
9. +10, +2
10. +5, +20

Page 27

1. 49, 48, 47, 46, 45, 44, 43, 42, 41, 40, 39
2. 98, 96, 94, 92, 90, 88, 86, 84, 82, 80, 78
3. 97, 94, 91, 88, 85, 82, 79, 76, 73, 70, 67
4. 96, 92, 88, 84, 80, 76, 72, 68, 64, 60, 56
5. 95, 90, 85, 80, 75, 70, 65, 60, 55, 50, 45
6. 94, 88, 82, 76, 70, 64, 58, 52, 46, 40, 34

Page 28

1. –10; 60, 50, 40, 30, 20, 10, 0
2. –10; 53, 43, 33, 23, 13, 3
3. –8; 68, 60, 52, 44, 36, 28, 20, 12
4. –5; 77, 72, 67, 62, 57, 52, 47, 42
5. –9; 64, 55, 46, 37, 28, 19, 10, 1
6. –11; 56, 45, 34, 23, 12, 1
7. –20; 120, 100, 80, 60, 40, 20, 0
8. –25; 200, 175, 150, 125, 100, 75, 50, 25

Page 29

1. 40, 38, 35, 33, 30, 28, 25, 23
2. 38, 37, 32, 31, 26, 25, 20, 19
3. 36, 32, 29, 25, 22, 18, 15, 11
4. 70, 65, 55, 50, 40, 35, 25, 20
5. 88, 86, 82, 80, 76, 74, 70, 68
6. 140, 130, 110, 100, 80, 70, 50, 40

Page 30

1. 10, 13, 12, 15, 14, 17, 16, 19
2. 10, 15, 13, 18, 16, 21, 19, 24
3. 11, 10, 14, 13, 17, 16, 20, 19
4. 26, 24, 34, 32, 42, 40, 50, 48
5. 14, 11, 17, 14, 20, 17, 23, 20
6. 40, 45, 35, 40, 30, 35, 25, 30

Page 31

1. +2, –3
2. +1, –5
3. +3, –1
4. +4, –2
5. –1, +5
6. –2, +3
7. –5, +2
8. –10, +2
9. –4, +9
10. +7, –2

Page 32

Answers will vary.

Page 33

Blocks should be circled in correct groups.

1. yes
2. yes
3. no
4. yes
5. no
6. no
7. no
8. yes
9. 1, 2, 4, 8

Page 34

Xs should be circled in correct groups.

1. yes
2. yes
3. yes
4. yes
5. no
6. yes
7. no
8. no
9. no
10. no
11. no
12. yes
13. 1, 2, 3, 4, 6, 12
14. 1 x 12; 12 x 1; 3 x 4; 4 x 3; 2 x 6; 6 x 2
15. 1, 2, 3, 4, 6, 12

Page 35

1. yes; no
2. no; yes
3. yes; yes
4. yes; no
5. no; yes
6. yes; no
Possible answers:
7. 1, 2, 3, 6, 9, 18
8. 2, 3, 4, 6, 8, 12, 24

Page 36

1. yes; no
2. yes; no
3. yes; yes
4. no; yes
5. yes; no
6. yes; yes
7.–8. Answers will vary.

Page 37

Multiplication table should be completed.

1. 20
2. 15
3. 35
4. 32
5. 54
6. 72

Page 38

birds: 4, 6, 8, 10, 12
cats: 8, 12, 16, 20, 24
bugs: 12, 18, 24, 30, 36
octopuses: 16, 24, 32, 40, 48

1. 12 legs	2. 20 legs
3. 24 legs	4. 48 legs
5. 16 legs	6. 36 legs
7. 24 legs	8. 36 legs

9. 3 cats; 2 bugs; 5 bugs; 2 octopuses

Page 39

Rotten Egg: 20¢, 30¢, 40¢, 50¢, 60¢
Skunk: 30¢, 45¢, 60¢, 75¢, 90¢
Moldy Berry: 40¢, 60¢, 80¢, $1.00, $1.20
Sour Milk: 50¢, 75¢, $1.00, $1.25, $1.50

1. 40¢	2. 60¢
3. 80¢	4. $1.00
5. $1.40	6. $2.10
7. $3.50	8. $4.20

9. 5 Moldy Berry; 3 Skunk; 3 Skunk; 5 Sour Milk

Page 40

eyes: 8, 12, 16, 20, 24, 28, 32, 36, 40, 44
teeth: 4, 6, 8, 10, 12, 14, 16, 18, 20, 22

1. 20 eyes	2. 18 teeth
3. 7 Xerks	4. 8 Xerks
5. 24 + 12 = 36	6. 40 + 20 = 60
7. 5 Xerks	8. 11 Xerks

Page 41

eyes: 3, 6, 9, 12, 15, 18, 21, 24, 27, 30, 33
horns: 4, 8, 12, 16, 20, 24, 28, 32, 36, 40, 44
teeth: 5, 10, 15, 20, 25, 30, 35, 40, 45, 50, 55

1. 15 eyes	2. 32 horns
3. 50 teeth	4. 7 Freeps
5. 9 Freeps	6. 7 Freeps
7. 15 + 20 + 25 = 60	8. 3 Freeps
9. 8 Freeps	

Page 42

stegosaurus: 100, 150, 200, 250, 300
tyrannosaurus: 150, 225, 300, 375, 450
triceratops: 200, 300, 400, 500, 600

1. $1.25   2. $4.00
3. $4.50
4. 4 tyrannosauruses; 6 triceratops
5. 6 tyrannosauruses; 10 stegosauruses
6. $8.00

Page 43

1. 50	2. 40
3. 65	4. 25
5. 100	6. 85
7. 109	8. 25

9. 15, 30, 44, 105, 52, 90
10. 15, 27, 45, 95, 30, 65
11. 8, 15, 36, 12, 59, 100

Page 44

1. 6	2. 5
3. 20	4. 4
5. 70	6. 5
7. 20	8. 7

9. 2, 4, 6, 8, 10, 12
10. 12, 30, 48, 24, 6, 60
11. 2, 5, 3, 10, 4, 1

Page 45

1. (14); 13	2. (17); 27
3. (5); 25	4. (12); 22
5. (3); 24	6. (30); 27
7. (10); 5	8. (5); 13
9. (15); 5	10. (24); 4

Page 46

1. (7), 14; (11), 22; (2), 4; (6), 12; (16), 32; (25), 50
2. (4), 20; (7), 35; (0), 0; (1), 5; (10), 50; (20), 100
3. (6), 3; (10), 5; (14), 7; (24), 12; (50), 25; (100), 50
4. (15), 3; (25), 5; (60), 12; (35), 7; (10), 2; (100), 20

Page 47

1. x2; (12); +3	2. −2; (6); x1
3. +1; (11); −3	4. +2; (6); ÷3

5. machines could both be 1, 2, or 3

6. +3; (10); x2	7. ÷3; (3); +2
8. −2; (10); x3	9. x3; (9); +1
10. ÷3; (5); x1	

Page 48

1. 6 + 3 = 9	2. 12 ≠ 6 + 5
3. 7 + 9 ≠ 15	4. 13 = 6 + 7
5. 9 + 8 = 17	6. 19 ≠ 8 + 10
7. 13 + 12 = 25	

Page 49

1. 5 + 2 = 1 + 6	2. 2 + 7 ≠ 4 + 3
3. 3 + 6 = 6 + 3	4. 2 + 3 ≠ 4 + 2
5. 5 + 3 = 4 + 4	6. 7 + 2 = 4 + 5
7. 4 + 3 ≠ 5 + 3	

Page 50
1. 6 = 4 + 2
2. 5 = 2 + 3
3. 3 + 4 = 7
4. 5 + 3 = 8
5. 9 = 2 + 7
6. 8 = 6 + 2
7. 4 + 6 = 10

Page 51
1. 5 = 3 + 2; 5 = 2 + 3; 2 + 3 = 5
2. 4 + 2 = 6; 6 = 2 + 4; 6 = 4 + 2
3. 7 = 5 + 2; 7 = 2 + 5; 2 + 5 = 7
4. 8 = 2 + 6; 6 + 2 = 8; 2 + 6 = 8
5. 9 = 4 + 5; 5 + 4 = 9; 9 = 5 + 4
6. 8 = 5 + 3; 3 + 5 = 8; 8 = 3 + 5

Page 52
1. 3 = 5 - 2
2. 6 - 4 = 2
3. 4 = 6 - 2
4. 7 - 5 = 2
5. 5 = 6 - 1
6. 1 = 5 - 4
7. 7 - 3 = 4

Page 53
1. yes
2. yes
3. no
4. yes
5. no
6. no
7. yes
8. yes
9. no
10. yes
11. yes
12. yes
13. no
14. yes

Page 54
1. yes
2. no
3. yes
4. no
5. yes
6. yes
7. no
8. yes
9. yes
10. no
11. yes
12. yes
13. yes
14. no

Page 55
1. Nate; 2; Kate; 2
2. Kate; 4; Nate; 4
3. Kate; 1; Nate; 1
4. Nate; 2; Kate; 2
5. Nate; 5; Kate; 5
6. Kate; 15; Nate; 15
7. Kate; 25; Nate; 25
8. Nate; 44; Kate; 44

Page 56
1.
2.
3.
4.

Page 56 (cont.)
1. 10
2. 10
3. 6
4. 8
5. 50
6. 72
7. 94
8. 118

Page 57
1. 4; 8 + 4 = 12; 12 - 4 = 8
2. 5; 6 + 5 = 11; 11 - 5 = 6
3. 3; 7 + 3 = 10; 10 - 3 = 7
4. 1; 10 + 1 = 11; 11 - 1 = 10
5. 2; 9 + 2 = 11; 11 - 2 = 9
6. 6; 4 + 6 = 10; 10 - 6 = 4

Page 58
1. 15 = ___ - 2; 17
2. 12 = ___ + 3; 9
3. 21 = ___ - 10; 31
4. 19 = ___ - 4; 23
5. 30 = ___ + 9; 21
6. 14 = ___ + 14; 0
7. 15 = ___ - 8; 23

Page 59
1. 8 x 6 = 48
2. 6 x 7 = 42
3. 4 x 9 = 36
4. 5 x 11 = 55
5. 12 x 7 = 84
6. 10 x 13 = 130
7. 8 x 12 = 96

Page 60
1. 40 ÷ 5 = 8
2. 64 ÷ 8 = 8
3. 54 ÷ 6 = 9
4. 36 ÷ 3 = 12
5. 50 ÷ 10 = 5
6. 90 ÷ 6 = 15
7. 100 ÷ 4 = 25

Page 61
1. 13 = 7 + 6
2. 25 - 15 = 10
3. 3 x 8 = 24
4. 18 ÷ 6 = 3
5. 35 = 5 x 7
6. 15 + 25 = 40
7. 4 x 6 = 24
8. 12 - 4 = 8

Page 62
1. picture should show 7 objects and 8 objects;
   7 + 8 = ___; 15
2. picture should show 6 objects and 4 objects;
   10 = 6 + ___ ; 4
3. picture should show 12 objects with 3 crossed out;
   12 - 3 = ___; 9
4. picture should show 15 objects with 9 crossed out;
   15 - ___ = 9; 6
5. picture should show 4 objects and 9 objects;
   ___ + 4 = 13; 9
6. picture should show 6 objects and 5 objects;
   ___ - 6 = 5; 11

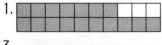

Page 63

1. picture should show 3 sets of 9 objects;
   $3 \times 9 = \_\_$; 27
2. picture should show 32 objects in groups of 4;
   $32 \div 4 = \_\_$; 8
3. picture should show 4 sets of 12 objects;
   $4 \times 12 = \_\_$; 48
4. picture should show 30 objects in 6 groups;
   $30 \div 6 = \_\_$; 5
5. picture should show 35 objects in groups of 7;
   $35 \div 7 = \_\_$; 5
6. picture should show 3 sets of 12;
   $3 \times 12 = \_\_$; 36

Pages 64-67

Answers will vary.

Page 68

1. $3 + 6 = 9$; $9 = 3 + 6$; $9 - 3 = 6$; $6 = 9 - 3$
2. $7 = 2 + 5$; $2 + 5 = 7$; $7 = 5 + 2$; $5 + 2 = 7$; $7 - 2 = 5$;
   $5 = 7 - 2$; $7 - 5 = 2$; $2 = 7 - 5$
3. $8 = 5 + 3$; $5 + 3 = 8$; $8 = 3 + 5$; $3 + 5 = 8$; $8 - 3 = 5$;
   $5 = 8 - 3$; $8 - 5 = 3$; $3 = 8 - 5$
4. $6 + 0 = 6$; $6 = 6 + 0$; $0 + 6 = 6$; $6 = 0 + 6$; $6 - 0 = 6$;
   $6 = 6 - 0$; $6 - 6 = 0$; $0 = 6 - 6$

Page 69-71

Answers will vary.

Page 72

1. 8×2; 4×4
2. 1×12; 12×1; 2×6; 6×2; 3×4; 4×3
3. 1×18; 18×1; 2×9; 9×2; 3×6; 6×3
4. 1×24; 24×1; 2×12; 12×2; 8×3; 3×8; 4×6; 6×4
5. 1×30; 30×1; 2×15; 15×2; 3×10; 10×3; 5×6; 6×5
6. 1×36; 36×1; 2×18; 18×2; 3×12; 12×3; 4×9;
   9×4; 6×6

Pages 73-75

Answers will vary.

Page 76

1. $4 \times 5 = 20$; $20 = 4 \times 5$; $20 \div 4 = 5$; $5 = 20 \div 4$
2. $6 \times 3 = 18$; $18 = 6 \times 3$; $3 \times 6 = 18$; $18 = 3 \times 6$;
   $18 \div 6 = 3$; $3 = 18 \div 6$; $18 \div 3 = 6$; $6 = 18 \div 3$
3. $7 \times 4 = 28$; $28 = 7 \times 4$; $4 \times 7 = 28$; $28 = 4 \times 7$;
   $28 \div 4 = 7$; $7 = 28 \div 4$; $28 \div 7 = 4$; $4 = 28 \div 7$
4. $9 \times 1 = 9$; $9 = 9 \times 1$; $1 \times 9 = 9$; $9 = 1 \times 9$; $9 \div 1 = 9$;
   $9 = 9 \div 1$; $9 \div 9 = 1$; $1 = 9 \div 9$

Pages 77-78

Answers will vary.

Page 79

1. $7 + 3 = 10$; $3 + 7 = 10$
2. $8 - 6 = 2$; $8 - 2 = 6$
3. $3 \times 4 = 12$; $4 \times 3 = 12$
4. $18 \div 3 = 6$; $18 \div 6 = 3$
5. $8 + 4 = 12$; $4 + 8 = 12$
6. $13 - 6 = 7$; $13 - 7 = 6$
7. $24 = 6 \times 4$; $24 = 4 \times 6$
8. $5 = 15 \div 3$; $3 = 15 \div 5$
9. $9 = 8 + 1$; $9 = 1 + 8$
10. $2 = 10 - 8$; $8 = 10 - 2$
11. $18 = 9 \times 2$; $18 = 2 \times 9$
12. $2 = 8 \div 4$; $4 = 8 \div 2$

Pages 80-81

Answers will vary.

Page 82

1. 2
2. 4
3. 6
4. 8
5. 10
6. 12
7. 14
8. 16
9. 18
10. 20
11. 22
12. 24
13. 26
14. 28
15. 30
16. 5
17. 7
18. 9
19. 11
20. 13
21. 15
22. 17
23. 14
24. 12
25. 11
26. 16
27. 15

Page 83

1., 2., 4., 5., 8., 9., 11., 13., 15., 16.: true
3. false; $5 + 9 = 5 + 5 + 4$ or $5 + 10 = 5 + 5 + 5$
6. false; $5 + 6 = 5 + 5 + 1$ or $5 + 7 = 5 + 5 + 2$
7. false; $6 + 8 = 6 + 6 + 2$ or $6 + 7 = 6 + 6 + 1$
10. false; $9 + 9 = 6 + 6 + 6$ or $9 + 6 = 6 + 6 + 3$
12. false; $4 + 7 = 4 + 4 + 3$ or $4 + 8 = 4 + 4 + 4$
14. false; $6 + 9 = 6 + 6 + 3$ or $6 + 8 = 6 + 6 + 2$

Page 84

1. 11
2. 12
3. 14
4. 13
5. 15
6. 17
7. 16
8. 18
9. 19
10. 20
11. 22
12. 21
13. 23
14. 35
15. 44
16. 13
17. 11
18. 15
19. 12
20. 17
21. 14
22. 16
23. 18
24. 23
25. 34

Page 85
The following should be circled: 1., 2., 3., 4., 5., 8., 9., 10., 12., 14., 15., 17., 19., 20., 21., 24.

Page 86
1. 9	2. 8	3. 2
4. 7	5. 5	6. 4
7. 3	8. 6	9. 1
10. 4 + 5; 5; 15		11. 6 + 1; 1; 11
12. 2 + 3; 3; 13		13. 1 + 6; 6; 16
14. 2 + 6; 6; 16		15. 5 + 2; 2; 12
16. 2 + 4; 4; 14		17. 1 + 8; 8; 18
18. 6 + 2; 2; 12		19. 7 + 2; 2; 12
20. 3 + 4; 4; 14		21. 1 + 7; 7; 17

Page 87
1. 5 + 4; 4; 24		2. 6 + 1; 1; 31
3. 5 + 2; 2; 42		4. 4 + 4; 4; 54
5. 3 + 6; 6; 66		6. 1 + 3; 3; 73
7. 2 + 4; 4; 84		8. 21
9. 42	10. 32	11. 54
12. 52	13. 73	14. 61
15. 26	16. 33	17. 42
18. 61	19. 86	

Page 88
The following should be circled: 1., 4., 5., 7., 10., 11., 12., 15., 16., 18., 19., 21., 22., 24.

Page 89
1. +	2. –
3. –	4. +
5. –	6. +
7. –	8. –
9. +	10. +
11. –	12. –
13. +	14. –
15. +	16. –
17. + or –	18. –
19. +	20. –

Page 90
1. =	2. ≠
3. ≠	4. =
5. ≠	6. =
7. =	8. ≠
9. =	10. ≠
11. ≠	12. ≠
13. ≠	14. =
15. =	16. ≠
17. ≠	18. =

Page 91
1. 12	2. 14	3. 37
4. 35	5. 57	6. 54
7. 37	8. 40	9. 5
10. 7	11. 6	12. 9
13. 17	14. 20	15. 27
16. 31	17. 18	18. 83

Page 92
1. true	2. true	3. false
4. true	5. true	6. false
7. false	8. true	9. true
10. true	11. false	12. true
13. true	14. false	15. true
16. false		

Page 93
1. 297	2. 298
3. 398	4. 398
5. 597	6. 190
7. 290	8. 390
9. 485	10. 585

Page 94
1. $2.97	2. $5.90	3. $11.85
4. $7.96	5. $4.95	6. $2.98
7. $6.90	8. $4.94	9. $4.94

Page 95
The following should be crossed out: 3., 5., 7., 9., 13., 14.

Page 96
1. =	2. ≠
3. =	4. =
5. ≠	6. =
7. =	8. =
9. ≠	10. ≠
11. ≠	12. =
13. ≠	14. ≠
15. ≠	16. ≠
17. =	18. =
19. =	20. ≠

Page 97

1. x	2. +	3. ÷	4. –
5. –	6. ÷	7. x	8. +
9. ÷	10. –	11. x	12. +
13. x	14. –	15. ÷	16. +
17. +	18. x	19. ÷	20. –
21. ÷	22. +	23. x	24. –

Page 98

1. 15	2. 11	3. 13
4. 16	5. 16	6. 18
7. 14	8. 14	9. 12
10. 17	11. 13	12. 15
13. 22	14. 25	15. 21
16. 22	17. 21	18. 24
19. 35	20. 33	21. 31
22. 41	23. 46	24. 44
25. 53	26. 52	27. 55

Page 99

1. 4	2. 4
3. 4	4. 2
5. 24	6. 45
7. 3	8. 5
9. 8	10. 2
11. 8	12. 8
13. 4	14. 7
15. 12	16. 14
17. 4	18. 9
19. 6	20. 15
21. 7	22. 8
23. 40	24. 16

Page 100

1. 7	2. 1
3. 6	4. 16
5. 3	6. 4
7. 6	8. 7
9. 30	10. 8
11. 1	12. 8
13. 5	14. 4
15. 1	16. 14
17. 5	18. 10
19. 4	20. 9
21. 18	22. 16
23. 8	24. 18

Page 101

1. 4	2. 0	3. 4	4. 1
5. 6	6. 0	7. 9	8. 1
9. 8	10. 0	11. 16	12. 1
13. 10	14. 0	15. 25	16. 1
17. 12	18. 0	19. 36	20. 1
21. 14	22. 0	23. 49	24. 1
25. 16	26. 0	27. 64	28. 1
29. 18	30. 0	31. 81	32. 1

Page 102

1. 8	2. 6
3. 4	4. 6
5. 14	6. 12
7. 2	8. 2
9. 3	10. 4
11. 18	12. 32
13. 13	14. 20
15. 2	16. 16

Page 103

1. 30 + 25 = 20 + 35
2. 30 – 15 = 25 – 10
3. 40 + 30 = 35 + 35
4. 60 – 15 = 75 – 30
5. 40 + 10 = 15 + 35
6. 50 – 25 = 60 – 35
7. 20 + 5 = 40 – 15
8. 25 + 25 = 75 – 25
9. 20 + 15 = 70 – 35
The problems should also be circled.

Page 104

The following should be circled:
1. 5 x 1; 2 + 3; 10 ÷ 2
2. 12 – 2; 20 ÷ 2; 5 x 2
3. 16 ÷ 2; 2 x 4; 5 + 3
4. 12 ÷ 2; 2 x 3; 6 ÷ 1
5. 20 ÷ 5; 10 – 6; 2 x 2
6. 21 ÷ 3; 6 + 1; 1 x 7
7. 9 ÷ 1; 3 x 3; 5 + 4
8. 10 – 9; 6 ÷ 6; 1 x 1
9. 12 ÷ 6; 18 ÷ 9; 10 – 8

Page 105

The following path should be followed: 6 + 6; 3 x 4; 13 – 1; 20 – 8; 6 x 2; 8 + 4; 12 ÷ 1; 7 + 5; 12 – 0; 18 – 6; 12 x 1; 11 + 1; 24 ÷ 2; 3 + 9; 36 ÷ 3

Pages 106-107

$5 \div 1 = 10 \div 2 = 15 \div 3 = 5 \times 1$
$48 \div 6 = 4 \times 2 = 16 \div 2 = 1 \times 8$
$24 \div 4 = 2 \times 3$
$7 \div 1 = 7 \times 1 = 49 \div 7 = 56 \div 8$
$36 \div 9 = 16 \div 4$
$6 \times 3 = 2 \times 9$
$3 \times 3 = 27 \div 3$
$24 \div 8 = 6 \div 2$
$4 \times 5 = 10 \times 2$

Page 108

A-F: all but bottom row of triangles should be shaded.
chart: C-9, 5; D-4, 16, 7; E-5, 25, 9; F-6, 36, 11
pattern: +3, +5, +7, +9, +11, +13; 16, 25, 36, 49

Page 109

A-F: all but bottom row and right column of squares should be shaded.
chart: C-9, 5; D-4, 16, 7; E-5, 25, 9; F-6, 36, 11
pattern: +3, +5, +7, +9, +11, +13; 16, 25, 36, 49

Page 110

chart: 3: 8; 4: 10; 5: 12; 6: 14; 7: 16
1. 5 tables
2. 9 tables
3. 10 people
4. 18 people
5. 14 people
6. 42 people
7. 202 people

Page 111

chart: 3: 14; 4: 18; 5: 22; 6: 26; 7: 30
1. 4 tables
2. 9 tables
3. 22 people
4. 42 people
5. 26 people
6. 82 people
7. 402 people

Page 112

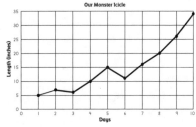

1. 2, 3; 5, 6
2. 2 in; 4 in; 4 in; 19 in; 5 in; 29 in
3. 1 in; 4 in
4. 9, 10, 8

Page 113

chart: 9, 14, 24, 11, 18, 13, 10, 11, 7, 18
1. Anchorage
2. Honolulu
3. Seattle
4. Denver
5. Honolulu & Miami
6. Anchorage
7. 70°F
8. Anchorage
9. Chicago & Washington, D.C.
10. 16, 33, 41, 42, 44, 45, 55, 62, 75, 75
11. 25, 51, 53, 57, 59, 59, 68, 80, 85, 86

Page 114

1. F − S = __
2. G + M = __
3. H + B = __
4. R − S = __
5. C − S = __
6. B + F + H = __
7. M − S = __

Page 115

1. H × W = __
2. N ÷ E = __
3. B × F = __
4. M ÷ S = __
5. R ÷ C = __
6. W × F = __
7. M × B = __

Page 116

chart: 3, 4, 5, 6, 7, 8, 9, 10, 11, 12, 13, 14
1. 2 games
2. 5 games
3. 15 games
4. 6 games
5. 13 games
6. 19 games
7. 97 games
8. 497 games
9. 103 games
10. 503 games

Page 117

chart: 1, 2, 3, 4, 5, 6, 7, 8
1. 4   2. 17   3. 15   4. 60   5. Answers will vary.
chart: 10, 9, 8, 7, 6, 5, 4, 3, 2, 1, 0
6. 7   7. 8   8. 1   9. 6   10. Answers will vary.

Page 118

A = 4, B = 2, C = 1; 1.−3. Answers will vary.
D = 5, E = 10, F = 1; 4.−6. Answers will vary.

Page 119

J = 5, K = 3, L = 4; 1.−3. Answers will vary.
4. The following should be circled: J + J + K = 13, K + K + L = 10, J − L = 1, J − 2 = K, 8 − J = K, L + 1 = J